ADVANCE PRAISE FOR

TROUBLING THE CANON OF CITIZENSHIP EDUCATION

"Richardson and Blades have assembled a book of richly provocative essays that challenges many of our complacent assumptions about civic education and suggests intriguing ideas for its revival in our schools. Their book will reward the attention of scholars and teachers alike."

Eamonn Callan, Professor of Education and Senior Associate Dean for Academic Affairs, School of Education, Stanford University

"Richardson's and Blades' edited collection offers an exciting and diverse synthesis of material placing 'citizenship' and 'citizenship education' at the centre of social and cultural inquiry. Not only do they extend the growing educational literature critiquing the canonical premises of citizenship and citizenship education. They also move beyond traditions that treat citizenship and citizenship education as solely derivative of the processes of democratization. The outcome is an extremely powerful and erudite set of texts that speak directly to the fallacies commonly associated with concepts such as citizenship and democracy in the 21st century. A serious 'must read' for anyone interested in understanding the limits of democracy in a globalizing world order."

Jo-Anne Dillabough, Associate Professor, Department of Educational Studies, University of British Columbia

TROUBLING THE CANON OF CITIZENSHIP EDUCATION

PETER LANG
New York • Washington, D.C./Baltimore • Bern
Frankfurt am Main • Berlin • Brussels • Vienna • Oxford

TROUBLING THE CANON OF CITIZENSHIP EDUCATION

GEORGE H. RICHARDSON
AND DAVID W. BLADES,
EDITORS

PETER LANG
New York • Washington, D.C./Baltimore • Bern
Frankfurt am Main • Berlin • Brussels • Vienna • Oxford

Library of Congress Cataloging-in-Publication Data

Troubling the canon of citizenship education /
edited by George H. Richardson and David W. Blades.
p. cm.
Includes bibliographical references.
1. Citizenship—Study and teaching. 2. Civics—Study and teaching.
3. Education—Aims and objectives. 4. Pluralism (Social sciences)
5. Civics, Canadian—Study and teaching. 6. Civics—Study and teaching—Canada.
I. Richardson, George H. II. Blades, David W.
LC1091.T76 370.11′5—dc22   2005020643
ISBN 0-8204-7605-6

Bibliographic information published by **Die Deutsche Bibliothek**.
Die Deutsche Bibliothek lists this publication in the "Deutsche
Nationalbibliografie"; detailed bibliographic data is available
on the Internet at http://dnb.ddb.de/.

Cover design by Dutton & Sherman Design

The paper in this book meets the guidelines for permanence and durability
of the Committee on Production Guidelines for Book Longevity
of the Council of Library Resources.

© 2006 Peter Lang Publishing, Inc., New York
29 Broadway, New York, NY 10006
www.peterlangusa.com

All rights reserved.
Reprint or reproduction, even partially, in all forms such as microfilm,
xerography, microfiche, microcard, and offset strictly prohibited.

Printed in the United States of America

To David, Lorraine, Benjamin and Simeon, may our children and grandchildren experience citizenship as a rich narrative, full of promise, commitment and action.

CONTENTS

Acknowledgments ix

David W. Blades and George H. Richardson
Introduction: Troubling the Canon
of Citizenship Education 1

PART I
Troubling Places for Citizenship Education

Alan M. Sears and Emery J. Hyslop-Margison
The Cult of Citizenship Education 13

Terrance R. Carson
The Lonely Citizen: Democracy, Curriculum, and
the Crisis of Belonging 25

Yvonne Hébert and Lori Wilkinson
Diversity and Democratic Values: Implications for Public Policy 31

PART II
Troubling School Subjects as Citizenship Education

Jennifer Tupper
Education and the
(Im)Possibilities of Citizenship 45

viii | Troubling the Canon of Citizenship Education

Hans Smits
 "Weak Ontology" as a Way of Reenchanting Citizenship
 in the Social Studies: A Memo with Some Random Notes 55

Jyoti Mangat
 Watch This [White] Space: Canadian Students Interrogating
 Citizenship and Identity 67

Ingrid Johnston
 Dislocating the Dominant Narratives of Citizenship
 in English Language Arts 76

PART III
Troubling Bodies in Citizenship Education

Kent den Heyer
 Defining Presence as Agents of Social Life and Change 85

Lori B. Macintosh and Lisa W. Loutzenheiser
 Queering Citizenship 95

William F. Pinar
 From Chattel to Citizenry: The Gender of the Law
 in the Sexual Politics of Race 103

PART IV
Troubling Visions of Citizenship Education

David W. Blades and George H. Richardson
 Restarting the Interrupted Discourse of the Public Good:
 Global Citizenship Education as Moral Imperative 115

David Geoffrey Smith
 Troubles with the Sacred Canopy: Global Citizenship
 in a Season of Great Untruth 124

List of Contributors 137

Index 141

ACKNOWLEDGEMENTS

Any edited collection is only as strong as its contributions. The editors would like to thank the different authors who contributed to this volume and applaud their willingness to take up our challenge to push the bounds of our thinking about citizenship education. We would also like to add a special thank you to Dr. Renee Fountain of Laval University for her important role in helping to conceptualize and organize the conference that was the genesis for this book.

David W. Blades and George H. Richardson

INTRODUCTION: TROUBLING THE CANON OF CITIZENSHIP EDUCATION

For the most part, the existing discourse of civic education has tended to privilege liberal democratic understandings of citizenship. Typically such understandings represent civic engagement as a series of rational, culturally neutral acts undertaken by individuals who conceive of citizenship and "the common good" in the fundamentally universalist terms (Dewey, 1916; Barber, 1992; Mogdil and Mogdil, 2000; Ravitch & Vitteritti, 2001; Englund, 2002). From this disembodied perspective, the influence of race, gender, sexual orientation, ethnicity, and socioeconomic status on citizenship is all but ignored (Greene, 1996; Torres, 1998; Apple, 2000; Arnot & Dillabough, 2000), and citizenship education itself emerges in a normative guise in which difference is suppressed in favour of the creation of "equality and symmetry" (Benhabib, 1996, 70).

Yet we know the civic community is neither equal, nor symmetrical. Rather, it represents, in Chantal Mouffe's terms, a "surface of inscription of a multiplicity of demands" (1995, 36) in which community, culture, identity, and class have significant impacts on how we construct and act out citizenship (Callan, 1997; Torney-Purta, 2001; Richardson & Blades, 2001; Kymlicka, 2001; Banks, 2004). As Maxine Green (1996) notes, such a dynamic understanding of citizenship suggests "a democratic community always is in the making . . . there always are newcomers, always new stories feeding into living history out of which a community emerges and is continually renewed" (42).

Furthermore, we also know that different cultures perceive and constitute concerns and risks in global issues differently and ask (and do not ask) different questions about citizenship (Stevenson, 2001; Richardson, Blades, Kumano & Karaki, 2003; Carlson & Dimitriadis, 2003; Banks, 2004). In terms of sexuality and gender, we know that in many societies gays and lesbians may not always experience the benefits of full citizenship, that women become citizens in a pattern different from that of men, and that they perceive civic issues differently than men (Wilson, 1995; Pinar, 1998; Yuval-Davis & Werbner, 1999; Arnot & Dillabough, 2000).

On a global scale, as economies worldwide become increasingly interdependent we know that citizens of the world face highly complex public policy issues that are more and more transnational in scope. In the face of the emergence of a new, global civil society there is a growing sentiment that citizenship education needs to be reconceptualized as an interdisciplinary, international dialogue (Kubow, Grossman & Ninomiya 1998; Merryfield, 2001; Richardson & Blades, 2003). Recent work in citizenship education has certainly taken up this imperative. For example, Cogan (1998) suggests that the traditional orientation of citizenship education "towards the development of a sense of national identity" no longer works well given "the complexity, scale and interconnectedness" (p. 1) of the challenges that face the world community in the 21st century. Selby and Pike (1995) emphasize the need to develop an international curriculum of world citizenship if we are to counter the negative effects of globalization.

Implicit in this call for a reconceptualized and expanded definition of contemporary citizenship education is the understanding that the civic community is so multifaceted, so diverse, that citizenship needs to be founded, on the notion that there exists "a plurality of ways of belonging" to a civic community (Taylor, 1993, 183).

Given these emergent understandings of the complex, plural, and dynamic quality of citizenship in contemporary society, it is of vital importance for scholars to look beyond the existing canon of citizenship education in search of new possibilities for civic education.

To encourage this search for new possibilities, this book has two distinctive features. The first is the diversity of the analytic frameworks and perspectives that are brought to bear on citizenship education. These frameworks are drawn from postcolonialism, feminism, critical theory, hermeneutics, queer theory, and poststructuralism. In terms of the wide-ranging perspectives from which citizenship education is examined, this collection incorporates race, gender, socioeconomic status, culture, and sexual orientation. The second distinctive feature is the essay-based structure of the work. Rather than present a series of descriptive or comparative studies of civic education practices, the essays in this collection are thoughtful engagements with the existing canon of citizenship education that, taken together, suggest how we might "enlarge the space of the possible" (Sumara & Davis, 1997) in civic education.

To that end, this volume brings together the work of sixteen Canadian and American curriculum scholars in a collective reimagination of the space of civic education. Together, these essays "trouble" existing conceptions of citizenship and seek to broaden the horizon of citizenship education.

In the context of our intention to be troublesome about citizenship education, we have organized the essays in this book around four interrelated themes. The first theme, "Troubling Understandings of Citizenship Education," asks us to consider the position and purpose of civic education. While it is true to say that from the outset of mass public education, education for citizenship has always been the central mandate of schools, it is also true to say that there are no clear understandings of what we mean when we speak of 'citizenship' or 'citizenship education' (Osborne, 1997; Lawson & Scott, 2002). Despite the fact that many scholars (Barber, 1984; Oldenquist, 1996; Sears, 1997; Parker, 2001) have expressed significant doubts about whether the inherently authoritarian nature of schools make them inappropriate locations for civic education, the last fifteen years have seen a proliferation of research on ways to improve and enhance citizenship education in schools.

Looking at this renewed emphasis on civic education, Alan Sears and Emery Hyslop-Margison ask whether citizenship education has assumed cult status. Drawing on the work of Janice Gross Stein (2001), Sears and Hyslop-Margison suggest that both right- and left-wing proponents of citizenship education have taken on some key characteristics of the promoters of religious cults, in particular: the incantation of simplistic and unsupported dogmas, the requirement of blind loyalty to these, and the demonization of those "on the other side."

As Sears and Hyslop-Margison point out, this kind of simplistic mantra is endemic to the history of educational reform but, in the end, not particularly helpful in producing substantial, lasting results. They argue that a more careful examination of the current state of citizenship and more nuanced understanding of how people become citizens is necessary to build the foundation for an effective citizenship education.

Building on their research on values in citizenship education, Yvonnne Hébert and Lori Wilkinson suggest that the concerns, confusion, and debate concerning citizenship values are linked to how we view social capital and cohesion as public policy tools. In an attempt to clarify some of these concerns, the authors examine the logical relationships between citizenship values, virtues, principles, dispositions, and concepts in the attempt to suggest an analytic framework to guide policy, research, and curriculum development.

Drawing on Gandhi's legacy of *ahimsa* and reflecting on Dewey's notion that schools and communities should be linked together in the process of educating for citizenship, Terry Carson asks how we, as educators, can act to create a democratic public in the public schools of Canada and the United States. As Carson notes, this question has taken on a particular urgency in the face of the social fragmentation, alienation, and extreme individualism that is a characteristic of advanced capitalist societies.

The second theme of the collection, "Troubling School Subjects as Citizenship Education," asks us to consider the current location of citizenship education in schools. Typically, citizenship education has been located in the humanities, however such subject area isolation belies the fact that citizenship is lived both in and out of classrooms of all sorts, and that *being* a citizen is much more than *learning about* citizenship. While there have been frequent calls (Jones & Jones, 1992; Cogan & Derricott, 1998; Oelkers, 2001) for an interdisciplinary approach to teaching citizenship, civic education, by and large, remains the responsibility of the humanities. If citizenship education is, in a sense, "bounded" by the humanities, what are the possibilities for reimagining how it might be understood and taught?

In response to this question, Jyoti Mangat discusses how the classroom use of literary texts can help promote an investigation of race—and more particularly "whiteness"—as it relates to students' ideals of citizenship and identity in contemporary, multicultural societies. Using a Canadian classroom as an example, Mangat examines ways in which students' responses to the short story, "The Management of Grief" by Bharati Mukherjee (1988) can be used to help students investigate their own assumptions and beliefs about citizenship and national identity.

Expanding on the use of literature in the context of citizenship education, Ingrid Johnston examines the ways in which language and literature are inextricably linked with notions of citizenship, society, and the ways we live with one another in the world. Johnston considers how contemporary English language arts classrooms can move beyond the historical view of subject 'English' as a civilizing force that promotes unity and shuts out differences. Instead, she advances that these classrooms may become the sites of new discourses that question the 'taken-for-granted' views of the past. Through a creative rereading of past 'classic' works and an exploration of contemporary texts Johnston suggests that students can expose the ideological nature of literary texts and allow for dialogue on the multiple ways we understand ourselves as citizens and members of a democratic community.

Focusing on the ideological foundations on which citizenship education is constructed and delivered in social studies, Jennifer Tupper explores the ways in which citizenship falls short in education and how we might reimagine it in order to create new possibilities for ways of being in the world. Informed by feminist theories of citizenship and democratic schooling, Tupper provides a critique of citizenship, which highlights both its inclusive and exclusive nature. Drawing on her own research with students and teachers and Ruth Lister's theory (1997) of "differentiated universalism," Tupper outlines the contours of a reimagined citizenship education that transcends the way citizenship is currently constructed and lived in schools.

Finally, Hans Smits asks us to consider how we might "reenchant" citizenship education through returning to foundational questions about what it means to be a citizen. Drawing on the work of Stephen White (2000), and reading White's work through contemporary literary texts, Smits asks, "What can sustain certain kinds of ontological beliefs about the self as citizen?" He uses White's articulation of a "felicitous weak ontology" as a basis for thinking about curriculum in interdisciplinary terms and examines how such terms may support a view of citizenship that has in mind a notion of practice that focuses on how to respond to and address others.

The third theme of the collection, "Troubling Bodies in Citizenship Education," asks whether the normative discourse of citizenship acts to restrict and constrain the horizons of civic education. In schools, as is the case in general society, we know that identities count and that bodies matter. The sheer diversity of the life experiences of students always resists the temptation to think of citizenship as the Same; always resists the seduction to the generic (Torres, 1998; Carlson & Dimitriadis, 2003). Yet in spite of this knowledge, citizenship education continues to be structured around the assumption that responsible citizenship consists of disembodied, dispassionate, rational engagements in the public sphere.

Taking up the question of how subjectivities affect the enactment of citizenship, Kent den Heyer notes the importance of agency as a crucial, if underutilized, second-order concept in social studies. Den Heyer argues that the question teachers and students ought to consider should not be the generic "what does it mean to be a citizen" but rather, the more individual "in what ways do people participate as agents in shared social-symbolic, political, and material worlds." In contrast to individuals and formal political action, den Heyer suggests the latter question broadens students' analyses to consider the multiple domains (e.g., formal political, familial, spiritual, economic) in which people work for, resist, or unknowingly participate in group struggles over the symbolic and material organization of social life. As evidence of the possibilities this questions holds for revitalizing citizenship education, den Heyer examines the relationship between individual agency, group struggles, and social change.

In their essay, "Queering Citizenship," Lori Macintosh and Lisa Loutzenheiser explore the intersections and disjunctures amongst queer theories, citizenships and curriculum theories, and examine the potential for a queered lens to disrupt curricular frameworks. Through their use of "queer" and "queering," and "queered," they force an extension beyond binaries of queer and not queer, a refiguring of identities containing unstable and always multiple and partial positions. By queering curriculum theories, Macintosh and Loutzenheiser set forth troubled categories that purposefully misalign with normative identity constructions, as an attempt to burst apart those traditional constructions. Their essay asks us to consider how thinking outside of citizen, gay or lesbian student, success or failure might be helpful in the reading and writing of education, pedagogy, and curricula.

In "The Civic and the Sexual," William Pinar asks how we can dedicate ourselves to educating citizens in a multicultural society when the very category of the civic is saturated with the sexual and when much of the debate in this area is taken up with investigating questions of "whiteness." But as he notes, once we settle on the term, the questions begin: What is the psychosexual structure and historical character of "whiteness" that renders it so aggressive, so tortured, so interested in subjugation? Is there something complex and elusive at work in the phenomenon beyond "prejudice" no matter how sophisticated our typology of that complex phenomenon becomes? In response to these questions, Pinar suggests that one answer is to radically restructure the civic to include the sexual.

The final theme for the collection "Troubling Visions for Citizenship Education" asks us to consider how we conceive of the purposes of civic education in an age of globalization. Traditionally, citizenship education has been bound to the interests of the nation state and realized in policy through systems of public education (Hahn, 1998; Torney-Purta, Schwiller & Amadeo, 1999; Heater, 2001). But despite what might be termed the "entrenched" culture of citizenship education, contemporary concerns and developments progressively call the traditional location and emphasis of citizenship education into question.

As economies world-wide become increasingly interdependent and as the international community confronts global issues ranging from planetary warming and rapid technological innovation to the dangerous rise of unilateralism on the part of the United States, the sheer complexity of these concerns demands that we think about the moral responsibilities of citizenship in different ways.

In our essay "Restarting the Interrupted Discourse of the Common Good: Global Citizenship as Moral Imperative," we examine the question of whether it is possible for students in different countries to engage in international, interdisciplinary conversations about the responsibilities of world citizenship. Conceptualizing and developing such conversations, however, raises complex issues. For example, what constitutes a common good for all humanity? What is the role of educational systems around the world in fostering the development of global citizenship? To begin to address these questions, we discuss a joint research project in which Japanese and Canadian researchers developed a two-year pilot that invited secondary school students to discuss the value of engaging in conversation about these issues with their counterparts in another country. In light of the encouraging results of the project, we suggest one way to develop a worldwide conversation about citizenship is by considering the metaphor of the *agora*, a place of provocative conversation where the everyday commerce of living can (in)form the development of a global imaginary of citizenship.

Finally, in his provocative contribution, "Troubles with the Sacred Canopy: Global Citizenship in a Season of Great Untruth," David Geoffrey Smith draws on recent biblical scholarship and the work of Argentine philosopher Enrique Dussel to engage in a rigourous critique of the "Christo-centric" theology of sacrifice and redemption that lies at the heart of European (and American) modernity. As Smith notes, this theology is as much responsible for current American foreign policy as it was for the justification for European expansion and imperialism in the period after 1492.

Arguing that our contemporary understandings of global citizenship are played out under this same "sacred canopy" of sacrifice and redemption, Smith poses an alternate construction for global citizenship based on what he terms a "Comparative Discourse of Empire." From a comparative perspective, he suggests, it is possible to learn to see Europe/America as only one empire within the world's long experience of imperial regimes. As Smith notes, such a perspective allows a more self-conscious fracturing of the sacred canopy so that the underlying assumptions of the empire can be jarred loose for a more profound critical investigation.

In the context of "troubling" the canon of citizenship education, these essays ask us to look beyond the normative liberal democratic discourse of civic education and, borrowing from Eamonn Callan, to imagine other possibilities for "creating citizens" (Callan 1998). In so doing, we want to stress the vital role schools have played and should continue to play in educating for democracy. But, as we hope these chapters suggest, democracy is best served when citizenship education truly reflects the plurality of voices and ideas that make up the complex fabric of civic society.

References

Apple, M. (2000). *Official knowledge: Democratic education in a conservative age* (Second Ed.). New York: Routledge.

Arnot, M., & Dillabough, J.-A. (Eds.). (2000). *Challenging democracy: International perspectives on gender, education and citizenship*. New York: Routledge.

Banks, J. A. (Ed.). (2004). *Diversity and citizenship education: Global perspectives*. San Francisco: Jossey-Bass Publishers.

Barber, B. (1984). *Strong democracy: Participatory politics for a new age*. Los Angeles: University of California Press.

Barber, B. (1992). *An aristocracy of everyone: The politics of education and the future of America*. New York: Ballantine Books.

Barney, D. (2000). *Prometheus wired: The hope for democracy in the age of network technology*. Vancouver: University of British Columbia Press.

Benhabib, S. (Ed.). (1996). *Democracy and difference: Contesting the boundaries of the Political*. Princeton, NJ: Princeton University Press.

Callan, E. (1997). *Creating citizens: Political education and liberal democracy*. New York: Oxford University Press.

Carlson, D., & Dimtriadis, G. (Eds.). (2003). *Promises to keep: Cultural studies, democratic education and public life*. New York: RoutledgeFalmer.

Cogan, John J. (1998). The challenge of multidimensional citizenship for the 21st century. In J. J. Cogan and R. Derricot (Eds.), *Citizenship for the 21st century: An international perspective on education* (pp. 155–167). London: Kogan Page.

Cogan, J. J., & Derricott, R. (Eds.). (2000). *Citizenship for the 21st century: An international perspective on education*. London: Kogan Page.

Cornwell, G. H., & Guarasci, R. (Eds.). (1997). *Democratic education in an age of difference: Redefining citizenship in higher education*. San Francisco: Jossey-Bass Publishers.

Dewey, J. (1916/1966). *Education and democracy*, New York: Free Press.

Englund, T. (2002). Rethinking democracy and education: Towards an education of deliberative citizens. *Journal of Curriculum Studies* 32(2), 305–313.

Feinberg, W., & McDonough, K. (Eds.). (2003). *Education and citizenship in liberal-democratic societies: Teaching for cosmopolitan values and collective identities*. New York: Oxford University Press.

Greene, M. (1996). Plurality, diversity and the public space. In A. Oldenquist (Ed.), *Can democracy be taught?* (pp. 27–44). Bloomington, IN: Phi Delta Kappa Foundation.

Hahn, C. (1998). *Becoming political: Comparative perspectives on citizenship education*. Albany, NY: State University of New York Press.

Heater, D. (2001). The history of citizenship education in England. *The Curriculum Journal 12(1)*, 103–124.

Hébert, Y. (2002). *Citizenship in transformation in Canada*. Toronto: University of Toronto Press.

Jackson, R. (Ed.). (2002). *International perspectives on citizenship education and religious diversity*. London: RoutledgeFalmer.

Jenkins, H., & Thornton, D. (Eds.). (1999). *Democracy and new media*. Cambridge, MA: MIT Press.

Jones, E., & Jones, N. (1992). *Education for citizenship: Ideas and perspectives for cross-curricular study*. London: Kogan Page.

Kubow, P., Grossman, D., & Ninomiya, A. (1998). Multidimensional citizenship: Educational policy for the 21st century. In J. J. Cogan and R. Derricot (Eds.), *Citizenship for the 21st century: An international perspective on education* (pp. 115–133). London: Kogan Page.

Kymlicka, W. (2001). *Politics in the vernacular: Nationalism, multiculturalism, and citizenship*. London: Oxford University Press.

Lawson, H., & Scott, D. (Eds.). (2002). *Citizenship education and the curriculum*. Westport, CN: Ablex Publishing.

Leicester, M., Modgil, S., & Modgil, C. (Eds.). (2000). *Politics, education and citizenship*. London: Falmer.

Lister, R. (1997). Dialectics of citizenship. *Hypatia, 12(4)*, 1–13.

Merryfield, M. (2001). Moving the center of global education: From imperial worldviews that divide the world to double consciousness, contrapuntal pedagogy, hybridity, and cross-cultural competence. In W. C. Parker (Ed.), *Critical issues in social studies education for the 21st century* (pp. 150–179). Greenwich, CT: Information Age Publishers.

Mouffe, C. (1995). Democratic politics and the question of identity. In J. Rajchman (Ed.), *The identity in question* (pp. 33–46). London: Routledge.

Oelkers, J. (Ed.). (2001). *Futures for education: Essays for an interdisciplinary symposium*. New York: Peter Lang.

Oldenquist, A. (Ed.). (1996). *Can democracy be taught?* Bloomington, IN: Phi Delta Kappa Foundation.

Osborne, K. (1997). Citizenship education and social studies. In I. Wright & A. Sears (Eds.), *Trends and issues in Canadian social studies* (pp. 39–67). Vancouver: Pacific Educational Press.

Parker, W. C. (2001). Toward enlightened political engagement. In W.B. Stanley (Ed.), *Critical issues in social studies research for the 21st century* (pp. 97–118). Greenwich, CT: Information Age Publishing.

Parker, W. C. (2004). *Teaching democracy: Unity and diversity in public life*. New York: Teachers College Press.

Pinar, W. F. (Ed.). (1998). *Queer theory in education*. Mahwah, NJ: Lawrence Erlbaum Associates.

Ravitch, D., & Viteritti, J. P. (Eds.). (2001). *Making good citizens: education and civil society*. New Haven, CN: Yale University Press.

Richardson, G. & Blades, D. (2001). Social studies and science education: Developing world citizenship through interdisciplinary partnerships. *Canadian Social Studies*, 35, 10 pp. http://www.quasar.ualberta.ca/css.

Richardson, G., Blades, D., Kumano, Y., & Karaki, K. (2003). Fostering a global imaginary: The possibilities and paradoxes of Japanese and Canadian students' perceptions of the responsibilities of world citizenship. *Policy Futures in Education 1(2)*, 402–420.

Sears, A. (1997). Social studies in Canada. In I. Wright & A. Sears (Eds.), Trends and issues in Canadian social studies (pp. 18–38). Vancouver: Pacific Educational Press.

Stevenson, N. (Ed.). (2001). *Culture and citizenship*. Thousand Oaks, CA: Sage.

Taylor, C. (1993). *Reconciling the solitudes: Essays on Canadian federalism and Nationalism.* Montreal: McGill-Queens University Press.

Torney-Purta, J., Schwiller, J., & Amadeo, J. A. (Eds.) (1999). *Civic education across countries: Twenty-four national case studies from the IEA civic education project.* Amsterdam: The International Association for the Evaluation of Educational Achievement.

Torney-Purta, J. et. al. (2001). *Citizenship and education in twenty-eight countries: civic knowledge and engagement at age fourteen.* Amsterdam: International Association for the Evaluation of Educational Achievement.

Torres, C. A. (1998). *Democracy, education and multiculturalism: dilemmas of citizenship in a global world.* Lanham, MD: Rowman & Littlefield.

Werbner, P., & Yuval-Davis, N. (Eds.). (1999). *Women, citizenship and difference.* London: St. Martin's Press.

Wilson, A. R. (Ed.). (1995). *A simple matter of justice: Theorizing lesbian and gay politics.* New York: Cassell.

I
TROUBLING PLACES FOR CITIZENSHIP EDUCATION

Alan M. Sears and Emery J. Hyslop-Margison

THE CULT OF CITIZENSHIP EDUCATION

Introduction

A recent report investigating the poor performance of New Brunswick students on international tests relative to their counterparts in Alberta, suggests that education reform in New Brunswick is driven by questionable ideological assumptions and commitments rather than reliable research and data analysis:

> Previously proposed solutions have typically represented one interest or another. They have been based on personal experience, and on personal commitment to one model or another. They have fueled the divisiveness of the situation to such an extent that few will now speak candidly about the issues or about appropriate solutions. Those who venture solutions, do so with personal and anecdotal information rather than with information about the whole system" (Scraba, 2002, n.p.).

A contemporary Ontario policy audit reached similar conclusions about educational reform in that province: "The provincial educational policies introduced over the six years were developed and enacted without much demonstrable attention to empirical evidence about what would improve teaching and learning" (Leithwood, Fullan & Watson, 2003, p. 24).

Of course, New Brunswick and Ontario are not alone in their tendency to introduce poorly conceived educational reforms. Hunt (2002) points out that the history of public education reform in the U.S. contains many similar examples of crusaders attempting to reshape curriculum on the basis of narrow ideological commitments: "they seem to believe that their salvific action alone will rescue the world of education from the forces of darkness and superstition, selfishness and traditionalism" (p. xvi). For example, the Soviet Union's launching of Sputnik in the late 1950s and the publication of *A Nation at Risk* in 1983 both prompted reactionary educational reform in the U.S.

The same discourse of crisis is often employed by ideologues to justify major educational reform in Canada. The federal government is particularly adept at using such language to rationalize its intervention in an area of provincial constitutional jurisdiction. In 1961, for example, Ellen Fairclough, Minister of Citizenship and Immigration, utilized cold war rhetoric to justify federal intervention in technical and vocational education: "The nations of the Western world are today faced with a gigantic struggle, on many fronts, with the world of Communism. Our best minds in the world of science and technology have not ceased to warn us that if we are to win the economic, scientific and intellectual struggle with Communism we must without delay apply ourselves to a sweeping new approach to education." (Fairclough, 1961, n.p.).

The perceived lack of support by immigrant groups for the war effort in the 1940s, massive postwar immigration in the 1940s and 1950s, rising tensions between French and English Canadians in the sixties and seventies, and the sense of exclusion among youth, women, cultural minorities, and persons with disabilities were all cast as crises justifying federal intervention in citizenship education. The language of crisis has become more pronounced over the years, and the state's interest in citizenship education as a vehicle to promote national identity and unity intensified accordingly (Sears, 1996).

In her 2001 Massey Lectures, *The Cult of Efficiency*, Janice Gross Stein (2001) suggests that this type of overheated rhetoric is ubiquitous in contemporary public discourse. She argues that public debate about health care and education in particular is overtaken by a cult mentality that precludes meaningful dialogue about effective reform. A cult mentality routinely commits to simplistic slogans and dogma while remaining unreflective about attending assumptions, implications, and alternatives. In this chapter we argue that much of the rhetoric and activity in the area of citizenship education reflects the cult mentality referred to by Stein. Although this pattern is endemic to the history of educational reform, it is notoriously unhelpful in producing substantial, lasting, or effective curricular change that understands and fosters democratic citizenship. We conclude by suggesting that a more careful and nuanced examination of citizenship education is required to understand and promote participatory democratic citizenship.

The Rise of Citizenship Education

Kymlicka and Norman (2000) point out that "the last ten years have witnessed a remarkable upsurge of interest in two topics amongst political philosophers: the rights and status of ethnocultural minorities in multiethnic societies, and the virtues, practices and responsibilities of democratic citizenship" (p. 1). Cairns (1999) similarly observes that, "the reawakening of scholarly interest in citizenship has been dramatic" (p. 3). Much current interest in citizenship is largely propelled by the sense of crisis we describe above. Indeed, a recent paper on voter participation produced by the Centre for Research on Information About Canada (2001) focuses on the question, "Is Canadian Democracy in Crisis?"

There is also an explosion of international interest and activity in citizenship education. The discourse of crisis and reform in democratic citizenship is revealed in the policies and curricula of national jurisdictions as diverse as Australia, Russia, Colombia, and Singapore. For example, the Civic Experts Group (1997) painted a bleak picture of Australian citizenship and citizenship education. In response, the government committed $25 million to develop and implement school programs in citizenship and to train qualified teachers for the field. In September of 1998 the English Advisory Group on Citizenship (1998), a blue ribbon panel commissioned by the Secretary of State for Education and Employment, was established "to provide advice on effective education for citizenship in schools" (p. 4). The group subsequently called for citizenship education to "be a statutory entitlement in the curriculum" (p. 22) and identified specific outcomes to guide the development of citizenship curricula and practice. This approach reflects a major departure from the British schooling tradition that regards citizenship education as a cross-curricular theme. Canada has yet to place citizenship education on the national agenda to the same extent as Australia and Britain, but there is considerable activity in this country as well. Citizenship and social cohesion are major themes in the Council of Ministers of Education Pan-Canadian Educational Research Agenda initiative, and there are significant curricular initiatives being implemented in some provincial jurisdictions (Sears, Clarke & Hughes, 1999).

In addition to these national initiatives, several supranational organizations have sponsored large-scale international efforts in the area of citizenship education. UNESCO launched an international comparative project, "What Education for What Citizenship," seeking "to formulate educational policies for citizenship education based on relevant and reliable empirical evidence" (International Bureau of Education, 1994, p. 1). The Council of Europe initiated an ambitious project on citizenship education for the new Europe with individual projects in most European countries and Quebec (Birzea, 2000). Since 1999 the Centre for Citizenship Education at the Hong Kong Institute of Education has been a leader in exploring the possibilities for democratic citizenship education in Asian societies (see, for example, Lee, Grossman, Kennedy, & Fairbrother, 2004).

The Language of Crisis in Citizenship Education

The degree to which a sense of crisis drives international reforms in citizenship education is striking. Citizens, especially young ones, are often described as: *ignorant* of the basic information required to function as citizens; *alienated* from politically participating in their societies; and *agnostic* because they supposedly do not believe in the values that support democratic citizenship. The Civics Expert Group in Australia coined the phrase "civic deficit" to capture the idea of pervasive ignorance among that nation's citizenry. The group reported that various commissioned studies "revealed a high level of ignorance about Australia's system of governments and its origins" (p. 132). The British Advisory Group on Citizenship also employs the language of deficit to describe citizens' knowledge of national history and government structures. More than fifteen years ago, Ravitch and Finn (1987) queried Americans on *What Do Our 17 Year Olds Know?* They concluded the answer was precious little and suggested sweeping educational reforms to correct this knowledge deficit. On major national holidays, the Dominion Institute inevitably reminds Canadians of our ignorance about national history, government, and contemporary culture. In response, wealthy Canadian families and foundations pour millions of dollars into curriculum projects to reclaim a supposedly lost Canadian identity.

The discourse of crisis is pervasive. In academic circles, eminent professors such Michael Bliss (1991) and Jack Granatstein (1998) worry respectively about the *Sundering of Canada* and *Who Killed Canadian History?* Peter Mansbridge (1997), perhaps English Canada's most recognized journalist, summed up the prevailing perspective during a lecture at the Centre for Canadian Studies at Mount Allison University when he proclaimed, "our ignorance is appalling" (p. 7). The mantra of citizen ignorance is typically used to support calls for education to emphasize the study of history and politics as prerequisites to effective citizenship. Although we support categorically the study of history and politics, there is little reason to believe that student knowledge of these subjects necessarily reveals successful citizenship education. Rather, such knowledge must be balanced with the dispositional requirements of meaningful political engagement. Unfortunately, the ideologues and organizations advancing the crisis of ignorance uniformly neglect this crucial element of citizenship preparation.

The crisis of alienation is more compelling than the crisis of ignorance. Carole Hahn (1998), reporting on data collected from students in four European countries and the United States, found high levels of citizen disengagement from politics. Torney-Purta, Schwille & Amadeo (2001) suggest that "countries find themselves with increasing numbers of adolescents who are disengaged from the political system" (p.14), and the British Advisory Group on Citizenship (1998) reports of a "potentially explosive alienation" (p. 16) from government institutions. In Canada, "voter turnout has declined in three straight federal elections" (Center for Research and Information in Canada, 2001, p. 4) reaching a record low in the federal election of 2000. While final numbers are not in for the 2004 federal election, concern about voter apathy prompted significant interest from news organizations and a program from Elections Canada titled "Student Vote 2004" intended to engage student interest in voting. One reason cited for alienation is widespread citizen disillusionment with corrupt or dishonest politicians. Hahn (1998) reports that in four of the five countries she studied less than 25% of students believe politicians could be trusted and in the fifth country (Denmark) only half said they could be trusted. She points out that "everywhere perceptions of honesty declined by about 20 percent from 1986 to 1993," (p. 29) and political scandals were a major contributor to this decline.

When citizens reject the principles of democracy or remain unconvinced about their possibility, there is a crisis of agnosticism. One Argentine colleague at a recent North American meeting implored, "don't teach us about the forms of democracy, we know all about the forms of democracy, we need to learn the spirit of democracy." Herman (1996) expresses the same sentiment about citizenship education in South Africa:

> The structures of democracy are necessary but not sufficient in themselves. Beyond a democratic constitution, the rule of law, and the mechanisms of universal suffrage, there must be an acceptance by the people of South Africa of the values and culture of democracy. (p. 189)

It is not enough to know about the structures and processes of democracy. Citizens must believe in democratic values and processes. For example, Gusseinov (1996) argues that a central challenge confronting democratic citizenship education in Russia is the "spiritual chaos" gripping Russian society. He believes it is essential to develop "a consensus among different social groups concerning the fundamental principles of its existence" (p. 167).

Hahn (1998) investigated the commitment of European and U.S. students to certain democratic rights. In particular, she examined the level of support for free speech and a free press. Her findings parallel other work in the field indicating that students express a high degree of support for these rights in the abstract. However, when these same values are applied to situations where students disagree with the expressed opinion their support declines significantly. Hahn contends that this equivocation on some of "the core principles of individual liberty and respect for all" is cause for concern and is not well addressed in citizenship education programs. Her school visits in the five countries suggest, "that educators have not given much deliberate attention to developing in students the capacity to extend fundamental freedoms and basic civil rights to groups that are the most disliked" (p. 175). The crisis of agnosticism is a driving force behind the growing emphasis in citizenship education programs to develop the values and dispositions of democratic citizenship.

The Crisis of Ignorance

The empirical evidence supporting the perceived crisis of ignorance facing citizenship and citizenship education is rather thin. McAllister (1998), an Australian political scientist writing about the so called "civics deficit" argues that "ever since mass opinion surveys first began to be used in the 1940s they have consistently shown that most citizens are anything but knowledgeable about politics. The majority know little about politics and possess minimal factual knowledge about the operation of the political system" (pp. 7–17). Osborne (2000) advances a similar view regarding the historical knowledge possessed by Canadians. While scholars such as Bliss and Granatstein contend there is a significant decline in knowledge of Canadian history, Osborne argues that available evidence does not support this view. He suggests that Canadians' lack of historical knowledge is not novel but has concerned educators and policy makers for more than a hundred years.

There is a second fundamental question related to the supposed crisis of ignorance: What is it, precisely, that Canadians do not know? The Dominion Institute initiated a series of surveys that received significant attention from the Canadian media. An analysis of some surveys conducted by the Institute raises concerns about their relevance to citizenship education. For example, one survey asked participants to identify actor Michael J. Fox as the Canadian on a list of various celebrities. Even questions that address political and historical knowledge more directly, including the name of the first Prime Minister or the names of the four original provinces, are not particularly essential to good citizenship. Does this mean we should not worry about the possible ignorance of Canadian citizens? No, but recognizing that such ignorance has persisted over many years and is often related to arcane historical and political facts reduces the sense of impending crisis. With the sense of crisis alleviated, there is more time to generate a substantive investigation on the degree and nature of citizen ignorance, how this lack of knowledge relates to citizenship, and what might be done to improve the situation.

The Crisis of Alienation

The voting rates, numbers of young people joining political parties, and levels of trust of politicians and public institutions indicate that many young citizens are in fact alienated from politics in both established and emerging democracies. Perhaps the critical indicator of this alienation is the worrisome decline in voting rates. As we noted above, Canadian voting rates have declined in three straight federal elections to a record low of 61% in the 2000 federal election and preliminary results indicate a new record low turnout for the federal election of June 2004. (Centre for Research and Information on Canada, 2001, Globe and Mail, 2004). This troubling pattern is reflected in democracies around the world with the most significant decline among younger voters. While much of the rhetoric in citizenship education attributes this decline to growing cynicism among young people, a closer examination of the evidence indicates a more complex situation. Surveys of young Canadians suggest, "they are no more cynical than older Canadians" (Centre for Research and Information on Canada, 2001, p. 1).

Buckingham (1999) believes there is a much more positive way of reading young people's political disengagement. That is, young people have good reason to be alienated from a system that does not take their involvement seriously. He suggests that the deficit may not rest with the young people but with a political system closed to meaningful consultation and participation. Hahn's (1998) interviews with young people in Britain seem to confirm this view. Young citizens cited being ignored and not being taken seriously by politicians as key factors in their alienation. Similarly, Chareka (2004) found Canadian youth not disposed to vote, seeing it as ineffective in terms of having a voice or making change. The Centre for Research and Information on Canada (2001) suggests that structural factors such as Liberal Party hegemony, the permanent voters list, and the First Past The Post election system might all contribute to young voter disaffection in this country. The centre argues that young people are no less alienated than their parents, but in the absence of political commitment are less likely to vote out of a sense of duty. Osborne (2000) summarizes these structural deficiencies by observing that, "the democratic deficit is the symptom of a structural problem that cannot be fixed through better citizenship education, but only through changes in the political system" (p. 126).

While Hahn (1998) and Chareka (2004) found students largely alienated from the formal political process they did not find them alienated from all forms of political participation. Young people in both studies were very willing to participate in community activities or in advocacy when they could see themselves actually making a difference. This finding is echoed in Gauthier's (2002) research on the political participation of Quebec youth, which concludes that while there is a definite drop in participation within traditional party politics there are clear signs of a developing new sense of what it means to be civically engaged: "despite commonly-held opinions, modern young people are far from apathetic. They are active at various levels of involvement in community life, although political partisanship is often suspect, even sometimes by those who officially belong to a political party."

Although longitudinal data from advanced industrial democracies reveal that, "there is clear evidence of a general erosion of support for politicians" and formal politics, there is also indication that one "response to popular dissatisfaction has been a move toward participatory democracy" (Dalton, 1999, p. 63). Social movements such as feminism, environmentalism, and, more recently, considerable opposition to global trade and monetary structures suggest an emerging grass roots form of citizen action. Protests against the war in Iraq brought millions of citizens into the streets worldwide. While reports indicate that protesters included a wide range of ages and social classes, many young citizens assumed leadership roles in organizing the rallies.

The Crisis of Agnosticism

What about growing concerns with the apparent lack of youth commitment to certain fundamental democratic values? Is it true that young citizens reject such basic democratic values as a respect for diversity, open mindedness, or a commitment to the common good? Glazer (1996) argues that fear of national disintegration lies at the heart of many recent public debates about American citizenship education. For example, some see recent efforts at inclusion, such as initiatives to introduce multicultural curricula, as undermining civic harmony. The same fear is reflected in Canadian educational debates and government policy decisions. The phrase *social cohesion* figures prominently in federal initiatives and the Council of Ministers of Education, Canada's (CMEC) Pan-Canadian Educational Research Agenda which identifies "Citizenship and Social Cohesion" as a central theme. In face of concerns about social disintegration, "social cohesion is invoked as a corrective measure that can help to increase social solidarity and restore faith in the institutions of government" (Joshee, 2004, p. 147). The desire to promote social cohesion implies an underlying fear that industrialized societies confront serious fragmentation in the face of economic globalization and growing cultural diversity. Citizenship education is often considered a bulwark against such decay.

Ethnically motivated attacks on foreign residents in Canada, Europe, and the United States might suggest a serious deficit of democratic values among young citizens. However, careful scrutiny indicates the situation is not that simple. Hahn (1999) reports that European and American students are very concerned about racism in their societies. So much so that they support limiting free speech and access to the press for identified racist groups. While one might argue that willingness to suppress basic rights for some groups is evidence of low levels of commitment to certain democratic values, it does demonstrate that many young people are genuinely concerned with ethno-cultural diversity, a fundamental requirement for the success of pluralistic democracies.

Canadian historian and nationally syndicated columnist Gwynne Dyer (2000) has written and lectured widely about how multicultural and immigration policies are successfully transforming Canada into a more diverse, tolerant, and more stable society. The IEA study reports very positive results related to students' acceptance of diversity. When asked if immigrants should have the opportunity to keep their own language, 77% of the students agreed or strongly agreed. On the question of being permitted to maintain their own customs and lifestyle, 80% agreed or strongly agreed and 81% felt immigrants should have the same rights as everyone else. Overall, the authors of the report on the study conclude that, "attitudes toward immigrants are generally positive" (Torney-Purta, Lehmann, Oswald & Schulz, 2001, p. 105). We do not suggest that there is no reason to be concerned about citizen commitment to the democratic values of open mindedness, tolerance, and respect and concern for the common good, but we believe the situation is far more complex than typically understood.

Conclusions and Recommendations

Generally, there is a paucity of evidence regarding what children and young people actually know about democratic citizenship, what their attitudes are, and what kinds of educational programs prove effective. Before developing and implementing sweeping reform, the development of knowledge within these areas is essential to citizenship education. A recent survey of Anglophone and Francophone college students in several regions of Canada investigated several citizenship areas: where do students find their sense of belonging, what are their attitudes toward diversity, and what is their level of civic engagement? The survey data is in the early stages of analysis, but it suggests a number of citizenship types that vary according to province, linguistic background, and gender (Pagé & Chastenay, 2003). Although it may be too early to make policy and curricular recommendations based on this research, young people seemingly practice citizenship in various ways and a "one-size-fits-all" approach may prove ineffective.

In June of 2002 the McGill Department of Political Science sponsored the workshop Citizenship on Trial: Interdisciplinary Perspectives on the Political Socialization of Adolescents. This event brought together political scientists, social theorists and educators from Canada, the United States, and Europe to share research relating to young people and citizenship. They investigated the relationship between youth involvement in community organizations and later civic activity. The assumption that community involvement enhances the civic knowledge, skills, and dispositions necessary for good citizenship is driving an explosion of interest in service learning across North America and elsewhere. Although there is clear evidence that young people engaged in civic participation are more likely to be engaged as adults, there is no evidence of a cause-and-effect relationship. This research may simply reflect the personality traits of those individuals who chose to participate in such acts. Regardless, citizenship education needs to stay connected to this growing body of work as new data emerge.

It is also critical to study how education shapes student knowledge, attitudes, and participatory dispositions related to citizenship. Officially, ministries of education across Canada declare schools the ideal place to formulate and express opinions to promote future democratic participation. Unfortunately, schools are rarely democratic institutions for either students or teachers. There is ample evidence that teachers resist dealing with controversial political issues in the classroom and that schools often discipline students who express concern about school policies or practices. David Brand, for example, was disqualified from participating in a school event because he protested his school's requirement that students watch a daily Youth News Network program. He reasonably concluded that, "school is not the place to have an opinion."

In spite of platitudes about preparing students for democratic citizenship, the general attitude of educators seems more consistent with Gene Hackman's character in *Crimson Tide*. Hackman, playing the captain of a nuclear submarine, says to his first officer "We are here to defend democracy, not practice it." Too often citizenship education in schools is sterile and designed to teach about democracy rather than practice it, and students "learn lessons different from the ones taught in their social studies class about exercising one's democratic rights." Education for democratic citizenship needs to model democracy, and schools must provide students with the dispositional qualities necessary to cultivate a far greater sense of political voice.

The cult mentality demanding reform in citizenship education is often based on dogma, reactionary ideological agendas, and the questionable crises of ignorance, alienation, and agnosticism. A more effective approach to reform should appreciate the complex and multifarious nature of democratic participation, view knowledge of history and politics as one element in a more sophisticated concept of citizenship, and understand the fundamental importance of fostering participatory dispositions in schools. Indeed, scholars in the field have a responsibility to provide deeper analysis about the various issues related to citizenship education and, in the words of Janice Gross Stein (2001), move the public conversation "from cult to analysis" (p. 192).

References

Advisory Group on Citizenship. (1998). *Education for citizenship and the teaching of democracy in schools*. London: Qualifications and Curriculum Authority.

Bliss, M. (1991). Privatizing the mind: The sundering of Canadian history, the sundering of Canada. *Journal of Canadian Studies*, 26 (4), 5–17.

Birzea, C. (2000). *Council for cultural cooperation: Project on Education for Democratic Citizenship: Education for democratic citizenship a lifelong perspective*. Strasbourg: The Council of Europe.

Buckingham, D. (1999). Young people, politics and news media: Beyond political socialization. *Oxford Review of Education*, 25, 171–175.

Cairns, A. (1999). Introduction. In Cairns, A. C., Courtney, J. C., MacKinnon, P., Michelman, H. J., & Smith, D. E. (Eds.), *Citizenship, diversity, & pluralism: Canadian and comparative perspectives* (pp. 1–22). Montreal and Kingston: McGill-Queens University Press.

Center for Research and Information on Canada. (2001). *Voter participation in Canada: Is democracy in crisis?* Montreal: Centre for Research and Information on Canada.

Chareka, O. (2004). Listening to the voices of African immigrants: A phenomenographic exploration of conceptions of political participation of recent African immigrants in comparison with those held by Canadians. Paper presented at the annual meeting of the Canadian Society for the Study of Education, Winnipeg, Manitoba, June 1, 2004.

Civics Expert Group. (1994). *Whereas the people . . . civics and citizenship education*. Canberra: Australian Government Publishing Services. CIVITAS. (2004). Retrieved May 20, 2004 from http://civnet.org.

Dalton, R. (1999). Political support in advanced industrial democracies. In Norris, P. (Ed.), *Critical citizens: Global support for democratic governance* (pp. 63). Oxford: Oxford University Press.

Dyer, G. (2000). He saved his country. *The Moncton Times and Transcript*. September 30, D 11.

Fairclough, E. (1961). Government and Education. A paper presented before the Business and Professional Women's Club, Sydney, N.S.

Foster, V. (1997). Feminist theory and the construction of citizenship education. In K. Kennedy (Ed.), *Citizenship education and the modern state* (pp. 126–136). London: Falmer Press.

Gauthier, M. (2002). The inadequacy of concepts: The rise of youth interest in civic participation in Quebec. A paper presented at Citizenship on Trial: Interdisciplinary Perspectives on the political socialization of adolescents, McGill University, Montreal, June 20–21.

Glazer, N. (1996). Five questions about multiculturalism. In A. Oldenquist (Ed.), *Can democracy be taught?Perspectives on education for democracy in the United States, Central and Eastern Europe, Russia, South Africa, and Japan* (pp. 9–25). Bloomington, IN: Phi Delta Kappa Educational Foundation.

Granatstein, J. L. (1998). *Who killed Canadian history?* Toronto: HarperCollins.

Gross Stein, J. (2001). *The cult of efficiency.* Toronto: Anansi.

Gusseinov, A. (1996). Education for democracy in Russia. In A. Oldenquist (Ed.), *Can democracy be taught? Perspectives on education for democracy in the United States, Central and Eastern Europe, Russia, South Africa, and Japan* (p. 167). Bloomington, IN: Phi Delta Kappa Educational Foundation.

Hahn, C. (1998). *Becoming political: Comparative perspectives on citizenship education.* Albany: State University of New York Press.

Herman, H. (1996). Education and the quest for democracy in South Africa. In A. Oldenquist (Ed.), *Can democracy be taught? Perspectives on education for democracy in the United States, Central and Eastern Europe, Russia, South Africa, and Japan* (p. 189). Bloomington, IN: Phi Delta Kappa Educational Foundation.

Hunt, T. C. (2002). *The impossible dream: Education and the search for panaceas.* New York: Peter Lang.

International Bureau of Education. (1994). *Experimental regional sub-projects on citizenship education.* Geneva: UNESCO.

Joshee, R. (2004). Citizenship and multicultural education in Canada: From assimilation to social cohesion. In Banks, J. (Ed.), *Diversity and citizenship education: Global perspectives* (pp. 127–156). San Francisco: Jossey-Bass.

Kymlicka, W., & Norman, W. (2000). Citizenship in Culturally Diverse Societies: Issues, Contexts, and Concepts. In Kymlicka, W. & Norman, W. (Eds.), *Citizenship in diverse societies* (pp. 1–44). Oxford: Oxford University Press.

Lee, W.O., Grossman, D. L., Kennedy, K. J., & Fairbrother, G. P. (Eds.). (2004). *Citizenship and Education in Asia and the Pacific: Concepts and Issues.* CERC Studies in Comparative Education 14. Norwell, MA: Kluwer Academic Publishers and Comparative Education Research Centre, The University of Hong Kong.

Leithwood, K., Fullan, M. & Watson, N. (2003). *The schools we need. Recent education policy in Ontario, recommendations for moving forward.* Toronto: OISE Press.

Mansbridge, P. (1997). *Canada's history: Why do we know so little?* Sackville: Centre for Canadian Studies, Mount Allison University.

McAllister, I. (1998). Civic education and political knowledge in Australia. *Australian Journal of Political Science, 33* (1), 7–17.

Osborne, K. (2000). Our history syllabus has us gasping: History in Canadian schools—past, present and future. *The Canadian historical review, 81* (3), 404–435.

Pagé, M. and Chastenay, M-H. (2003). Citizenship Profiles of Young Canadians. *Canadian Diversity/é cannadienne, 2(1),* 36–38.

Ravitch, D., & Finn, C. E. (1987). *What do our 17 year-olds know? A report on the first national assessment of history and literature.* New York: Harper & Row.

Scraba, E.J. (2002). *Schools Teach, Parents and Communities Support, Children Learn, Everyone Benefits: A Report on the New Brunswick Education System, Anglophone Sector. Advice to Dr. Dennis J. Furlong, NB Minister of Education* (Edmonton: Educational Consulting International, April 24, 2002). Downloaded from the internet, January 27, 2003 Http://www.c.../artikkel?&Dato = 20021209&kategori = ADS06&lopnr = 212090097&REF = A.

Sears, A. (1996). State Policy in Citizenship Education, 1947–1982. Unpublished doctoral dissertation, University of British Columbia.

Sears, A., Clarke, G. M., & Hughes, A. S. (1999). Canadian Citizenship Education: The Pluralist Ideal and Citizenship Education for a Post-Modern State. In Torney-Purta, J., Schwille, J., & Amadeo, J. (Eds.), *Civic education across countries: Twenty-four national case studies from the IEA education* project (pp. 111–136). Amsterdam: IEA.

Torney-Purta, J., Lehmann, R., Oswald, H., & Schulz, W. (2001). *Citizenship and education in twenty-eight countries: Civic knowledge and engagement at age fourteen.* Amsterdam: IEA.

Torney-Purta, Schwille, J., & Amadeo, J. (1999). *Civic education across countries: Twenty-four national case studies from the IEA education project.* Amsterdam: IEA

Terrance R. Carson

THE LONELY CITIZEN: DEMOCRACY, CURRICULUM, AND THE CRISIS OF BELONGING

In March 2003 a public symposium was held at the University of Alberta to explore the crisis in representative democracy. Among the speakers at the symposium–which was entitled "Escape from Politics"–was the President of the University of Alberta's Students' Union, who had achieved some notoriety in the 2000 Federal Election by forming the Edible Ballot Society. He and five other members of this society were arrested for eating their ballots as a demonstration of the futility of voting in a system that, regardless of the party you vote for, is not truly representative of the people. He argued that they wanted to make a statement "to get people to question democracy" (Kosowan, 2003, 3).

Whatever we may think of the gustatory gesture, the feeling that political parties do not speak for the average person is widespread. The futility of the ballot is reinforced by a general impression that politicians, of whatever political stripe, become indistinguishable from one another once they get into office. Indeed, the power of elected governments to act now seems to be increasingly circumscribed by transnational corporate power and global trade frameworks like NAFTA* and the World Trade Organization. All of this leads to a growing cynicism about the effectiveness of participating in the electoral process, especially among young people, who unlike their parents, have not developed the habit of voting. Youth voting rates reflect disaffection of many young people from the present system. In the 2000 Canadian federal election only 22% of eligible voters born after 1960 bothered to cast a ballot,

---

*Editor's note: North American Free Trade Agreement.

while 80% of older voters did. This percentage of youth vote remained about the same in the 2004 federal election, despite special appeals to young voters to exercise their franchise. Canada is not alone in having generally declining participation in the electoral process, particularly among young people. Participation in the 2004 American presidential election reflects a very similar trend, with young voters being among the least involved in the electoral process. Given the concerns already being raised about a growing "democratic deficit," this trend is clearly a worrying one for the future health of democracy, at least in its present form.

The fact that young people seem to be alienated from the formal political process, at least in terms of the procedural politics of present forms of representative government, speaks directly to educators: What is our responsibility? How should we, as teachers and curriculum theorists, begin to reimagine citizenship on the landscape of a growing crisis in representative democracy? One beginning place is a critical interpretive inquiry that questions how the present school curriculum and educational practices form the subjectivities of those who are becoming citizens. When we look at the present state of public schooling it is easy to see how a spirit of competitive individualism underwrites curriculum and teaching. The goal is to achieve good grades in high status subject areas, which are thought to lead to careers in business, engineering, and medical sciences. The curriculum itself is fragmented into specialist subject areas where the arts, humanities, and social sciences have increasingly become marginalized, crowded out by math, science, and technology. Responsibility for formal citizenship education is consigned largely to one subject area—social studies—but here it is mostly about history and the structures and functions of government, far removed from engagement in actual public issues that incite debate and require participatory democratic decision making. Too often the issues that really engage the attention of youth, such as personal safety, the environment, and social justice are not discussed, and when they are, the ways of getting involved are pretty much limited to voting and writing letters to the members of parliament.

If we think of curriculum etymologically, as "currere" (from the infinitive form of the Latin verb "to run"), meaning "to run" the course of one's life (Pinar, 1973), we are bound to inquire after the kind of person that is being formed running the course of such a fragmented curriculum. We might venture to say that such a person will most likely be a lonely and self-interested individual, one who is drawn by appeals to personal interests and likely resentful of the demands of community and of having to respond to what Michael Ignatieff (1984) has termed, "the needs of strangers." This person will have understood well that the world is an uncertain, insecure place that is fraught with dangers. One must make their way in such a world by becoming equipped with the necessary skills, knowledge, and attributes that will enable the person to ride out the vicissitudes of a chancy future. The self-interested individual bears an enormous responsibility for personal success; they learn that an array of career choices lies open to them, but they also come to appreciate the instability and inherent insecurity of those choices. The new economy and global competition for jobs and markets mean that one should not count on setting down roots anywhere. Can such a person be anything more than just nominally a citizen of the place where they happen to reside for the time being, a place in which they have only the most tenuous of attachments to a larger collectivity?

The condition of the lonely disconnected citizen, produced by a fragmented and narrowly instrumentalist school curriculum, is a far cry from the progressive educators' dream of public schools becoming "laboratories of democracy." That dream probably found its best expression in John Dewey's *Democracy and Education*, published in 1916. In this book Dewey famously declared that the task of the public school is not to educate people for democracy, rather it is to "create a democratic public" that will support and sustain democratic community. In making this important distinction Dewey, unlike many of his contemporaries, saw beyond the instrumentalist purposes of public schooling. He understood that the achievement of democracy is a matter of building relationships with others in particular environments; one becomes a democratic person with others and not through the personal acquisition of knowledge, skills, and attributes possessed by the individual citizen.

But when we consider the contemporary relevance of Dewey's idea that schools might become places for creating a democratic public, we must take note of how the community has changed in the intervening years. Dewey's remarkably productive life spanned the last half of the nineteenth century and the first half of the twentieth. He died in 1952 at the age of ninety-four. Dewey traveled widely, and although his writing and teachings influenced many educators throughout the world, his philosophical roots are thoroughly grounded in the soil of America and in American pragmatism. Dewey's reference point for democratic community was the material culture of late nineteenth- and early twentieth-century America, a time before mass ownership of private automobiles, the shopping mall, and ubiquitous personal entertainment systems of today's North America.

In his novel *Ragtime*, a recollection of 1906 America, E. L. Doctorow vividly describes the character of the public space of Dewey's day, a public space that is crowded with people living in close contact with one another. Teddy Roosevelt was president. The population customarily gathered in great numbers either out of doors for parades, public concerts, fish fries, political picnics, social outings, or indoors in public meeting halls, vaudeville theatres, operas, and ballrooms. There seemed to be no entertainment that did not involve great swarms of people. Trains and streamers and trolleys moved with them from one place to another. That was the style; that was the way people lived (Doctorow, 1975, pp. 3–4).

Without doubt Doctorow is giving us a nostalgic view of a golden past. I do not mean to valorize the past in this way but his description points to a certain loss of community or a sense of belonging to a place that is no longer a part of public life. It is an image of a world that we see now only in the old photographs of Jasper Avenue in Edmonton or Barrington Street in Halifax at the turn of the 20th century. These pictures, too, show great gatherings of people at public events in numbers that we can scarcely believe when we recall that, at the time, there were probably fewer than 100,000 people living in each of these cities.

Contrast these images of the crowded collectivity that marked the public space at the beginning of the last century with the highways, parking lots, and shopping malls that border our lives. In North America we now have a material environment that has essentially been constructed around the private automobile and has become emblematic of what Albert Borgmann (1992) has termed the "commodious individualism" (p. 6) that underwrites modernism. The public space has, itself, become more like a collection of privatized lives; a privatization of the life-world that has been made possible by a proliferation of home entertainment systems, personal computers, and an overarching culture of individualism.

Educational philosopher Maxine Greene reminds us of another difference between the public space in contemporary North America and the public space of Dewey's day. Greene points out that not only did Dewey and his contemporaries feel a boundless confidence that society could be rationally changed, they spared little thought for "gender difference or cultural diversity or even class divisions as factors relevant to education and public life" (1996, p.33). Greene calls attention to our present awareness that the community is now marked by a deep diversity and notes that there is a struggle for voice among those previously marginalized in a Eurocentric and patriarchal dispensation.

Given that the shape of the community is now very different, in twenty-first century North America, we educators must think again what it means to create a democratic public for this time and place, a time and a place in which the idea of "the public" has become expanded to include those previously marginalized. But it is also a much less optimistic time, some would say that the public space has become so privatized and so fragmented that they see little hope for meaningful participatory change. Low voter turnout can be taken as a clear sign of this cynicism, but it is also cynicism that is matched by governments themselves. As Canadian political scientist Reg Whitaker argued at the Escape from Politics symposium, "it is significant that the left and right have tried to move their important issues out of the reach of democratic politics and thus out of the reach of democratic accountability" (see Kosowan, 2003, p. 3). An even more worrying trend of governments is the active suppression of dissent in the interests of national security and the war on terrorism.

We seem to face heavy odds. But teachers should not give up; we should not become accomplices to the deepening cynicism about democratic politics. We might begin, for the moment, by rejecting the idea of democratic citizenship as mere abstraction. Instead, we should begin to listen to what a significant number of young people say about missing a sense of meaning and a feeling of belonging in school. These students are beginning to sense a certain nihilism in the curriculum, which treats education as a product to be consumed in the interests of career preparation for an endlessly deferred future. I noticed this several years ago when the Director of the Mahatma Gandhi Foundation in India came to the city of Edmonton. He was invited to speak at one of the large academic high schools in the city. The organizers were surprised that over 400 students came to the presentation, on very short notice. The students listening attentively and engaged the speaker from India with many probing questions about Gandhi's life and the relevance it might have for the contemporary world. What was the attraction for these students for a man like Gandhi, who fought for something called *swaraj* (self-rule) not in the sense of national independence for India, but as a rule of the self? As one of the teachers perceptively observed, "these students find meaning in Gandhi's project, they live in a world that is awash in information, but they are starved for meaning."

Gandhi is mainly known today for his message and practice of *satyagraha,* or nonviolent action. Satyagraha literally means "truth-force," and is found in the wisdom traditions of many religions and ancient teachings. For Gandhi the explicit origin of truth-force lay in the concept of *ahimsa*, which he drew from Jainism, the religion of his mother. According to the Jain teachings, we are born into this world of *himsa* (literally "harm"). The task of becoming human is to follow the practice of ahimsa, the practice of removing harm. Gandhi taught that removing harm meant not only abjuring direct violence but also addressing the structures or practices that cause harm to both the human and the natural world. Gandhi described his project in his autobiography as "my experiments with truth;" it is a reflective, open project that stands in sharp contrast to the path of fundamentalism, which has the solutions worked out in advance.

The wisdom traditions provide some critical insight into the sources of our problems with citizenship. At its heart the crisis of citizenship is an ontological problem, it is a crisis of meaning and a crisis of belonging. What most of the wisdom traditions, such as Buddhism, Confucianism, and First Nations spirituality, have in common is a belief in a reciprocal relationship between the cosmos and human beings. Growing up in one of these traditions involves becoming initiated into the great conversation about life and meaning. The conversation does not originate with the individual, nor is the individual left on his or her own to work out their relationship with the world as if it were purely a matter of personal goal setting.

We have placed an incredible burden on young people to make individual choices without having any other reference points except some chimerical ideal of personal success. As educator William Rees (2002) recently observed, surely citizenship means more than becoming a single-minded consuming machine. But what is it? I'm not sure that we actually know, at least not in any way that shows up meaningfully in the school curriculum. Reimagining citizenship involves a recovery of meaning, a reoccupation of a public space that has for too long been abandoned to individual self-interest. Is it any wonder the young cannot find themselves in a public space that is essentially empty?

We cannot return to some kind of nostalgia for community, nor can we take for granted that we now have one, if young people are abandoned to make what they will of their lives. Gandhi showed a path in his life not by just radically rejecting colonial rule –he said that he did not "simply want to exchange British rule for Indian rule"– but by creatively reworking of a deep tradition that was founded upon humane governance. He was only partially successful, India became a country like any other modern state and while the memory of Gandhi is honored, his teachings are largely ignored. Nevertheless, we educators need to keep refreshing a larger communal purpose in life, like the example of Gandhi or Martin Luther King, Jr.

Of course, one of the chief dangers now is fundamentalism: to confuse the image with the purpose. As James Hollis points out, "such literalism bewitches fundamentalists of all stripes when they seek refuge within the limits of their images rather than recalling that a sacred image points beyond itself toward the invisible" (2003, p. 83).

References

Borgmann, A. (1992). *Crossing the postmodern divide*. Chicago: University of Chicago Press.
Dewey, J. (1966). *Education and democracy*. New York: Free Press. (original published 1916)
Doctorow, E. (1975). *Ragtime*. New York: Random House.
Greene, M.(1996). Plurality, diversity, and the public space, in A. Oldenquist (Ed.), *Can democracy be taught?*, pp. 27–44. Bloomington, IN: Phi Delta Kappa Educational Foundation.
Hollis, J. (2003). *On this journey we call our life*. Toronto: Inner City Books.
Kosowan, E. Democratic process leaves a bad taste. *University of Alberta Folio*, April 4, 2003, 3.
Pinar, W. (2004). *What is curriculum theory?* Mahwah, NJ: Lawrence Erlbaum Publishers.
Rees, W. (2002). *The ecological footprint*. A presentation to the John Humphrey Conference on Human Rights, University of Alberta, Edmonton, April 2002.

Yvonne Hébert and Lori Wilkinson

DIVERSITY AND DEMOCRATIC VALUES: IMPLICATIONS FOR PUBLIC POLICY*

The question of values is one that reoccurs periodically in policy and educational circles. Today however, this question is raised within a global context experiencing rapid political, economic, social, and religious change (Turner, 2000). This question is at the heart of an intense and complex dynamic typical of democratic societies that are pluralistic, secular, and postmodern. The values debate today calls upon us to define what kind of world we want.

Canada is known to be a diverse society, notably in linguistic, cultural, and religious terms, resulting from the impact of policy changes sensitive to increasing immigration (Troper, 2002) and nations within the country (Hébert & Wilkinson, 2002; Kymlicka, 1995). In recent years, the values debate has become sharper and more acrimonious, especially in school contexts (McAndrew et al, 1997; Desaulniers, 2000). Generally speaking, students themselves are bearers of values which they construct upon social and familial experiences, and administrators and educators are confronted daily with decisions to make regarding the best possible response to conflicts of values that occur in educational institutions. In a context of globalization marked by the blurring of the frontiers and greater interconnectivity, the question of diversity and values in citizenship policy calls into review the pedagogical dimension of education.

---

*This research was supported by research grants from the Social Trends Project of the Social Sciences and Humanities Research Council of Canada, and from the Prairie Centre of Excellence for Research on Immigration and Integration.

This chapter serves as a starting point for clarifying the values debates with respect to democratic education from a global perspective. It can also be used to begin conversations about common human values, such as respect, that transcend nationality, culture, and heritage. This will move the debate away from focusing on which values constitute a unique Canadian identity and towards a more thought-provoking discussion of issues that contribute to patterns of conflict and paths of peace. This ethical and conceptual framework of democratic values including those inherent to diversity also avails itself to research on how values are lived and learned, to pedagogical and programmatic possibilities, and to policy development, be these social, political, or educational.

Understanding the Diversity and Values Debate

What do we mean, however, when we talk of *values*? Like the term *citizenship*, the concept of value is complex, multidimensional, and has multiple ramifications depending upon the views of individual actors, theoretical perspectives adopted, and specific objectives being considered. There is considerable confusion about a variety of terms used to talk about *values*, including such words as *principles, dispositions,* or *virtues*, often taken as equivalent terms. In other cases, values are taken up in a very broad way and refer indiscriminately to the development of a moral code, the recognition and respect of diversity, or the respect of human rights.

A debate rages about the values held by Canadian students and adults, their understandings of diversity, activism, and citizenship, as well as those held worldwide. Despite these tensions, many Canadians feel that a shared value system is important, and some of the current public anxiety may be traced to changes in these values (cf., Environics Research Group, 1994). Yet there is a growing split between the decision-making elite in Canada, who tend to emphasize economic-materialistic values, and the general public, who consider humanistic and idealistic values, such as freedom, a clean environment, a healthy population, integrity, individual human rights, safety, and security, as more important (Ekos Research, 1997). Furthermore, a pan-Canadian survey found that citizens share many values, among which figure importantly, self-reliance, children as an investment in the future, collective responsibility, and a desire for greater social equality among citizens (Peters, 1995). In light of this debate, a framework of logical relations is greatly needed with which to examine the relationship between values, diversity, and multiple discourses and notions of citizenship, so as to inform research, policy, and democratic education insightfully.

Defining Values, Principles, Dispositions, and Concepts

Understandings of the term value vary greatly and have evolved over time. In the 17th century, the term referred to the merit, qualities, or interest for which a person, idea, painting, literature, or music was esteemed (Rey, 1997). The original meaning is retained today in phrases such as the "value of a musical note" and the "aesthetic value of a painting," which bring in notions of weight and measurement. This meaning includes the idea of personal judgment of moral values and assumes a scale of values as a tool for measurement. Today, the term has sociological meaning, referring to systems of social values based on judgment and societal norms. Values are defined as referring to a constellation of ideals relating to democratic citizenship, which may be manifested as principles, dispositions, and concepts. Deeply held, *democratic values* have individual and social meaning, as well as cognitive, affective, and moral dimensions (Evans, Gräbler, & Pouwels, 1997).

Principles are a set of basic moral rules that define personal conduct. The term includes the notion of being in first place, of founding elements, of primary source, motive, and cause (Rey, 1997). Consequently, principles refer to foundational elements of general scope that logically constitute a science or discipline. The term principle also refers to normative rules of moral action, formulated explicitly or not, to which a person or group is attached and which flow from dominant values in a given society.

Democratic dispositions are best distinguished from values, referring to inclinations whereas the other terms refer to fundamental ideals. Democratic dispositions are thus defined here as acquired inclinations to engage with others, in altruistic ways that are consistent with underlying democratic values and principles. In other words, dispositions are a developed capacity to understand, accept, and act on the core principles of democratic society (Galston, 1991, 245–246). The meaning of disposition also includes the notion of arrangement, of being in good state and spirit as in "divine disposition," and of good will, taste, and aptitude (Rey, 1997). These are different than concepts, which originally referred to thought and to conception. Over time, concepts have come to refer to dynamic schematas of thought, rather than static configurations of notions (Rey, 1997).

Four Domains of Citizenship

The recognition of developmental stages of democratic citizenship is part of the ideas of T. H. Marshall who identified the evolution of civil, political, and socioeconomic rights as three domains of citizenship: civil, political, and socioeconomic (1998, 19). Since then, a fourth domain of citizenship has since emerged in reference to the culture-state relationship. We take up the four domains here as we wonder how values are linked to rights which have served, in the period since World War II, as a central focus for thinking about democracy and how such thinking is challenged by complex notions of pluralism.

The *civil domain* includes freedom of speech, expression, and equality before the law, as well as the freedom of association and access to information. Civil citizenship refers to a way of life wherein citizens define and pursue commonly held goals that are related to liberal conceptions of society on how common spaces, resources, and opportunities are shared and how interdependence is managed. Fundamental community values, limits of governmental decision making in relation to the individual citizen as well as the rights of private interest groups and associations are inscribed in the civil domain of citizenship which deals with the balance between individual and group concerns.

The *political domain* involves the right to vote and to political participation. Free elections are central to this dimension of citizenship, as is the right to freely seek political office. The civic dimension of citizenship understood as legal status defined in terms of rights and obligations of individuals, is a more confined notion than the civil domain and, in Marshall's view, flows more properly from the rights and responsibilities of the political and social domains.

Referring to the relationship between individuals in a societal context and requiring relational loyalty and sincerity, the *socio-economic domain* of citizenship refers to rights of participation, in political spaces, in the definition of social and economic rights, such as the rights to economic well-being, for example, the right to social security, to work, to minimum means of subsistence, and to a safe environment. Given the dynamic nature of Marshall's conception of citizenship,

> the constituent components of modern citizenship—civic responsibility, social trust, egalitarianism and a world-oriented individualism—cannot be viewed as static and isolated. (Kalberg, 1993, p. 107)

This perspective recognizes the complex interaction between the political, civil, and socioeconomic components and the implications for citizens within a global context.

Set within the culture-state relationship, the *cultural domain* refers to the manner in which societies take into account the increasing cultural diversity in societies, diversity due to a greater openness to other cultures, to global migration, and to increased mobility. Included in this domain is the quest for recognition of collective rights for minorities which, in Canada, are those of multinational groups, i.e., Francophones and Aboriginal First Nations who were *in situ* before the legal establishment of the federated state, as well as multicultural rights (Kymlicka, 1995), all set within the *Canadian Charter of Rights and Freedoms* (1982). The culture-state relationship is based upon human rights which recognize an anthropological dimension of the person, and which imply a certain conception of human beings, their dignity, and the affirmation of legal equality against all forms of discrimination on the basis of membership in a particular group or category. Particularly contentious, the culture-state relationship is hotly debated in Europe and North America.

Understanding Values and Diversity in Logical Relationship

In developing an analytic framework of democratic values, based on the Canadian sociological, survey, and educational literature, we explore logical relationships between values, principles, dispositions, and concepts by schematizing them and by representing them spatially. In doing so, we adopt the four domains discussed above as organizational framework and, in response to critiques of the Marshallian model, expand and complete this model of rights-focused citizenship with their complementary values. The first level of network organization is represented by a central category, democratic values proper, radiating out into a set of macroconcepts from the overarching concept (see Figure 1). In turn, each of these values leads to other levels of interrelated logical organization. In this way, democratic principles form the second level of schematization, dispositions a third, and concepts a fourth. Although the diagram below does not indicate directionality, it may be assumed that these all flow from democratic values, but

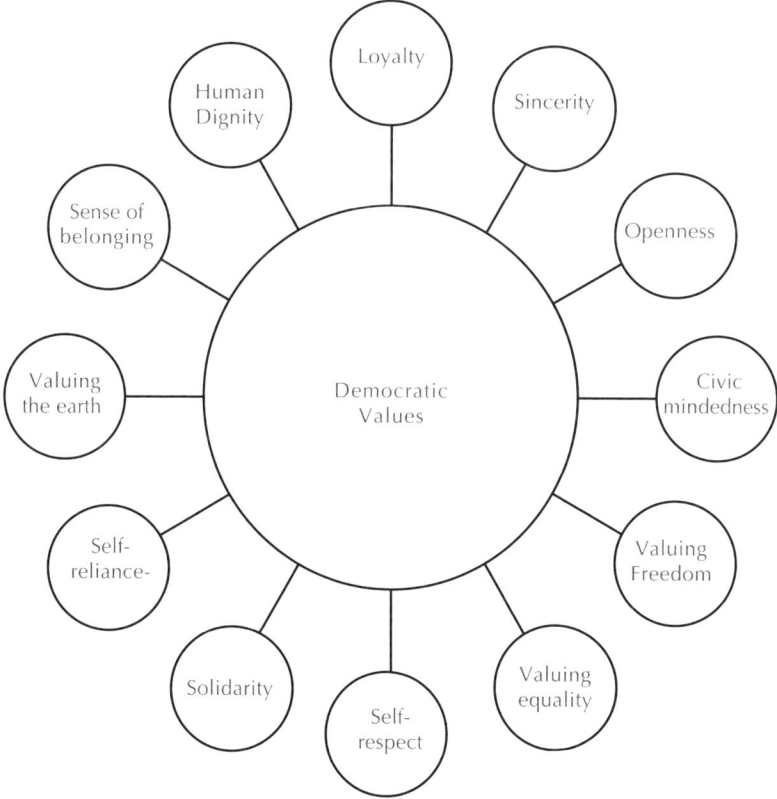

FIGURE 1: Twelve Macrovalues for Canada and Liberal Democratic Societies

also that they interrelate with each other, across level and from level to level, in logically inclusive relationships, thus reflecting the complexity and multidimensionality of democratic values. Serving as heuristic devices, the figures are not intended as quantitative measurements of values, but as a spatial representation, which allows for a visual account of the interrelationships between different levels of democratic values.

The essence of Figure 1 are the macroconcepts, twelve fundamental democratic values consisting of *loyalty, sincerity, openness, civic-mindedness, valuing freedom, valuing equality, respect for self and others, solidarity, self-reliance, valuing the earth, a sense of belonging,* and *human dignity.* Situated in a first circle, logical relationships may be read between them. For example, sincerity contributes to respect for self and others, just as valuing freedom contributes to being equal, to solidarity, and to a sense of belonging, and so on. Similarly, logical relationships may be read, from the center of the wheel, to each macroconcept, as these are in an 'is-a' relationship. In other words, self-reliance is a democratic value, as is human dignity, and civic-mindedness, and so on.

Serving as supraordinate organizers of a network of democratic values in four clusters, the four domains (civic, political, socioeconomic and cultural) inform the schematization of three other levels of logically inclusive relationships, though only one, *the cultural domain,* is discussed in depth here. In presenting the elements of the schematic structure of the analytic framework, we support their identification as a democratic value or related principle, disposition, or democratic concept, i.e., as second-, third-, or fourth-order democratic values.

Network of Democratic Values in the Cultural Domain

Given its recency, two democratic values are identified to date within the cultural domain, which is fewer than in the other three domains. Represented in Figure 2 below, a sense of belonging and human dignity are key values in the cultural domain as they are predicated upon a view of individuals, not merely as political or legal entities, but upon the recognition of the social and cultural nature of human beings (cf., Pouwels, 1997).

A sense of belonging assumes the existence of collectives, be these groups, communities, or the state, and thus of collective responsibility (Marzouk et al, 2000, Peters, 1995) as a citizenship principle which reflects social cohesion in that looking after others strengthens the well-being of society. In other words, Canadian society would be stronger if we collectively look after one another. Seemingly contradictory, the values of self-reliance and collective responsibility nonetheless co-occur in a dynamic tension. It is not possible for an individual to be entirely self-reliant, free, and separate from community, since to be an individual presupposes a community in which true freedom is intermeshed. The tensions between the two create the civil, political, social, and cultural institutions, which sustain

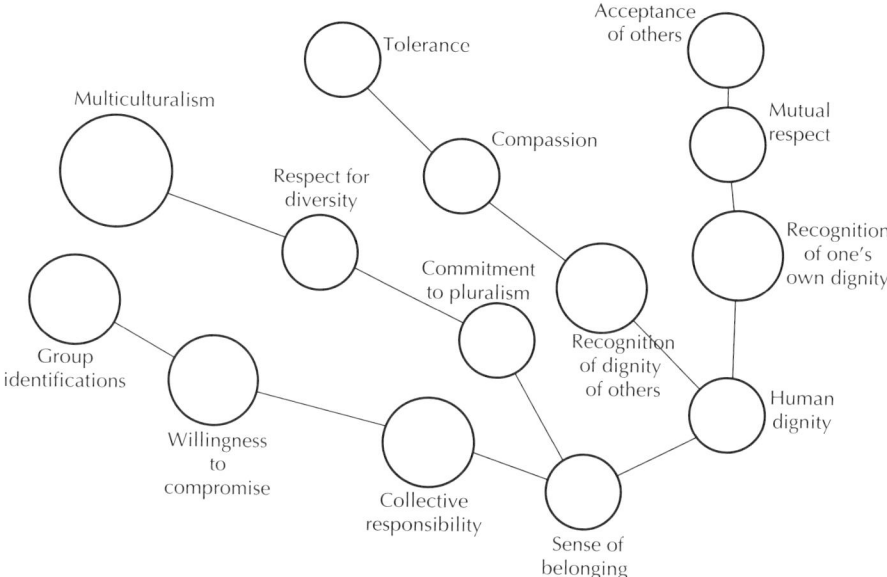

FIGURE 2: Network of Democratic Values in the Cultural Domain

both our freedom and satisfy our need to belong to something greater than ourselves. To actualize our collective responsibility, a willingness to find new solutions and to compromise is needed as a citizenship disposition, in logical relationship to categorical rights to group identifications, be it as national, religious, social, or other kinds of groups.

The value placed on human dignity requires a principled recognition of the dignity of others and of one's own, as well as a commitment to pluralism (Kymlicka, 1995; Pagé, 1997; Hemon, 1997; Lessard et al, 1997; Magsino, 2002; Bourgeault et al, 2002). This commitment is implied by the valuing of one's place(s) as part of collectivity which, in its turn, assumes and involves a distinction between individual and collective rights, a distinction which is based upon the recognition of the plurality of contemporary society. In a pluralist conception, civil engagement is as necessary and obligatory as social, economic, and cultural participation which can lower the barriers that divide society into minority and majority groups, going beyond group and individual identifications. These principles feed the recognition and respect of diversity, characteristic of a contemporary pluralist society such as Canada, as well as mutual respect and compassion for others. And finally, the value on human dignity, manifested as a principled recognition of others and of self, as well as a commitment to pluralism, acted upon in the form of mutual respect and of compassion, flows from and into democratic concepts of multiculturalism, tolerance, and acceptance of others.

Diversity and Values as Public Policy

Current federal policy concerns place democratic values at the very core of building a cohesive society which involves an "ongoing process of developing a community of shared values, shared challenges and equal opportunity within Canada, based on a sense of trust, hope and reciprocity among all Canadians" (Maxwell, 1996). Derived from investments in human, social, and cultural capital, this view considers social programs as well as civic engagement as fundamental to putting into place the trust and reciprocity, quality of life, and absence of social strife, needed to generate wealth (*Canadian Identity, Culture and Values,* 1996, 2). "Canada's success in the next millennium will hinge largely on the degree to which it can nurture, over the long term, a set of shared values and symbols. Moreover, the globalization of cultural expression will require that we continue to build common 'communities of interpretation'. This implies improved access to Canadian cultural content as an essential means of bridging linguistic, regional, and cultural differences and promoting common understanding" (3). While the dependence upon shared values that are regarded as legitimate and binding may be misinterpreted as a call for a simpler, more homogeneous society, the recognition of the inequities and exclusions of Canadian life is fundamental to moving towards redistributive social justice and critical multiculturalism (Baeker, 2000; Jenson, 1998; May, 1999).

Public policy concerns around diversity have been augmented with an interest in social capital as a public policy tool. Social capital involves the social networks and shared norms that facilitate collective action (Policy Research Initiative, 2004a). The networks and norms of social capital have long been an element of important public policy objectives in various areas including health, family well-being, economic development, crime and justice, immigrant integration, and civic participation (PRI, 2003). Inherent to social capital, shared norms may well include shared values especially as these pertain to civic participation and public education. There is a clear need for a better operational understanding of social capital in order to develop public policy that can promote optimal social and economic outcomes and address the state of civic institutions in Canada (PRI, 2004b, 2003).

Future Directions: Policy Development and Democratic Education

Collecting and organizing the wide variety of literatures on citizenship conceptually, as does this chapter, is but one step of many in better understanding the nature of values held by Canadian citizens. Nonetheless, it is important to recognize the contribution of conceptual work to the field. In response to critiques of Marshall's evolutionary stages of human rights, the analytic framework expands and completes rights-focused citizenship with complementary values.

Research is needed on the impact of notions of multiple, postmodern citizenships upon values as well as on the current state of democratic values, flowing from the analytic framework, so as to inform both policy development and democratic education. Understanding how citizens define values for themselves, how they live their values in daily life, how they resolve the tensions when these conflict, how young citizens live and learn values in the classroom, would illuminate the state of knowledge of values considerably.

Postmodern theories pose serious problems for the development of shared common values, perceived as key to a cohesive yet diverse citizenry. Some research questions to be examined include: How do democratic values, developed since antiquity and within modernity, fit contemporary Canadian society that is postmodern, multicentric, multinational, and polyethnic? How well do unitary citizenship policies forwarded by governments fit the multiplicity of realities and recognize a largely disunified yet multiple definition of citizenship? Most importantly, how does inclusion of a broad cultural dimension affect Canadian citizenship values and principles (Hébert, 2002, 1997) as they are practiced, individually and in institutions?

The fundamental set of democratic values proposed in the analytic framework to ensure a healthy democracy holds promise for policy development. Research is needed, however, to determine the current state of adherence to and applicability of these values. In other words, to what extent do Canadians hold these values and what they do when they conflict? How do citizens deal with the tensionality between values, such as those between liberty and solidarity? How do unrecognized, covert citizens' values interact with overt values? How are values defined, negotiated, and shared by Canadian citizens, as an entity, as members of diverse groups, and as individuals? What is the nature of the relationship between these values and Canada's political institutions and processes? How do various forms of citizenship engagement put into practice the citizenship values of the analytic framework? How does values education serve the preparation of future citizens? What new solutions, modifications, or recommendations flow from the analytic framework itself?

Intended to guide future research and policy development, these questions will not be easy to answer, nor will they be devoid of contention. True to the nature of plural and contested notions of citizenship, attempting to develop a policy framework that builds social capital and cohesiveness upon values will be challenging. The near future requires us to recognize the importance of the contentious socio-economic and cultural domains as part of citizenship in a plural society. A further challenge lies in being able to implement this ideal in policies, laws, and educational practices that adequately recognize all persons as individuals and as members of groups situated within all four domains of citizenship.

Citizenship today transcends the frontiers of the local community, the province or the national territory. From this flows the idea of being a citizen of the world and contributes to an emphasis on global education, human rights, and peace education. Thus, whether democratic education programs are specific or transversal, they aim to raise citizens' awareness of global issues, of different perspectives and to prepare them to act and interact with other citizens of the world to protect the environment, to struggle against inequalities and to preserve cultural lives, identities, artifacts, and symbols.

References

Baeker, Greg (2000). *Cultural policy and cultural diversity in Canada*. A report prepared for the Council of Europe's Study of Cultural Policy and Cultural Diversity. Reference: SRA-468. Ottawa: Department of Canadian Heritage.

Bourgeault, G., Gagnon, F., McAndrew, M, & Pagé, M. (2002). Recognition of cultural and religious diversity in the educational systems of liberal democracies. In Y. Hébert (Ed.), *Citizenship in transformation in Canada* (pp. 81–92). Toronto: University of Toronto Press.

Canadian identity, culture and values: Building a cohesive society. (1996). A Challenge Paper prepared for the ADM's Policy Research Committee. Ottawa: Canadian Heritage, Citizenship and Immigration, Canada; Human Resources Development Canada; Justice; Industry Canada.

Desaulniers, M.-P. (2000). École, valeurs et laïcité: vers de nouvelles approches du mieux vivre-ensemble. *Éducation Canada*, 40 (1), 33–37.

Douglass, R. B., Mara, G. M., & Richardson, H. S. (Eds.), *Liberalism and the good*. New York: Routledge.

Ekos Research (1997). *Rethinking government*. Ottawa: Canadian Heritage.

Environics Research Group (1994). *Focus Canada*. Ottawa: Canadian Heritage.

Galston, W. (1991). *Liberal purposes*. Cambridge: Cambridge University Press.

Hébert, Y. (1997). Citizenship education: Towards a pedagogy of social participation and identity formation. *Canadian Ethnic Studies*, XXX (2), 92–96.

Hébert, Y. & Wilkinson, L. (2002). The citizenship debates: Conceptual, policy, experiential and educational Issues. In Y. Hébert (Ed.), *Citizenship in transformation; Issues in education and political philosophy* (pp. 3–36). Toronto: The University of Toronto Press.

Hemon, E. (1997). De l'éducation à la paix à l'éducation mondiale. *Revue des sciences de l'éducation*, XXII (1), 77–90.

Jenson, J. (1998). *La cohésion sociale : l'état de la recherche au Canada*. Ottawa: Réseau canadien de recherche en politique publique.

Kalberg, S. (1993) Cultural foundations of modern citizenship. In B. S. Turner (Ed.), *Citizenship and social theory* (pp. 103–117), London: Sage Publications.

Kymlicka, W. (1995). *Multicultural citizenship: A liberal theory of minority rights*. Oxford: Clarendon Press.

Lessard, C., Desroches, F., et Ferrer, C. (1997). Pour un monde démocratique: l'éducation dans une perspective planétaire. *Revue des sciences de l'éducation*, XXII (1), 3–16.

Magsino, R. (2002). The debate between liberalism, communitarianism, republicanism and critical theory. In Y. Hébert (Ed.), *Citizenship in transformation: Issues in education and political philosophy* (pp. 57–80). Toronto: University of Toronto Press.

Marshall, T. H. (1998). Citizenship and social class. In S. Gershon (Ed.), *The citizenship debates: A reader* (pp. 93–112). Minneapolis: University of Minnesota Press.

Marzouk, A., Kabano, J., et Côté, P. (2000). *Éducation à la citoyenneté à l'école: Guide pédagogique*. Montréal: Les Éditions Logiques.

Maxwell, J. (1996). *Social dimensions of economic growth*. Eric John Hanson Commemorative Conferences, Vol. VIII, University of Alberta. Ottawa: Canadian Policy Research Network.

May, S. (Ed.) (1999). *Critical multiculturalism: Rethinking multicultural and antiracist education*. London/Philadelphia: Falmer Press.

McAndrew, M., Jacquet, M., & Ciceri, C. (1997). La prise en compte de la diversité culturelle et religieuse dans les normes et les pratiques de gestion des établissements scolaires: une étude explorative dans cinq provinces canadiennes. *Revue des sciences de l'éducation*, 23 (1), 209–232.

Pagé, M. (1997). Pluralistic citizenship: A reference for citizenship education. *Canadian Ethnic Studies*, 29 (2), 22–31.

Peters, S. (1995). *Exploring Canadian values: Foundations for well-being*. CPRN Study No. F-01. Ottawa: Canadian Policy Research Network.

Policy Research Initiative (2003). *Social capital as a public policy tool*. Downloaded May 16, 2003, *http://policyresearch.gc.ca/page.asp?pagenm=rp_sc_index*.

Policy Research Initiative (2004a). *The opportunity and challenge of diversity: A role for social capital?* Synthesis Report on an International Conference held November 23-25, 2003 in Montréal.

Policy Research Initiative (2004b). *Expert workshop on the measurement of social capital for public policy*. Synthesis Report, June 8, in collaboration with Statistics Canada.

Pouwels, J. (1997). Values education in the Netherlands In D. Evans, H. Gräbler, & J. Pouwels (Eds.), *Human rights and values education in Europe: Research in educational law, curricula and textbooks* (pp. 191–202). Fillibach Verlag Freidburg im Briesgau: European Commission.

Rey, A. (1997). *Le Robert, Dictionnaire historique de la langue française*. 2e édition. Paris: LE ROBERT.

Troper, H. (2002). The historical context for citizenship education in Urban Canada. In Y. M. Hébert (Ed.), *Citizenship in transformation in Canada* (pp. 150–161). Toronto: University of Toronto Press.

Turner, Brian S. (2000). Citizenship and political globalization: A review essay. *Citizenship Studies*, 4 (1), 81–86.

II
TROUBLING SCHOOL SUBJECTS AS CITIZENSHIP EDUCATION

Jennifer Tupper

EDUCATION AND THE (IM)POSSIBILITIES OF CITIZENSHIP

Introduction

Naming this chapter *Education and the (Im) Possibilities of Citizenship* reveals what I believe are the inherent tensions of citizenship education in schools and, in particular, social studies classrooms. In describing citizenship as both possible and impossible, I am suggesting that it occupies a space of uncertainty and ambiguity in education even though it attempts to pass itself off as definite and unmistakeable. Citizenship operates in schools to espouse a vision for students and teachers of what is "good" and "responsible" without really interrogating the concept itself. Thus, many students leave their classrooms without fully understanding the (im)possibilities that both inhibit and foster meaningful social and political participation. Impossible citizenship denies or ignores the false universalism embedded in liberal democracies and as such fails to cultivate a deep understanding of inequities that exist in the world. It creates "universal" conditions for citizenship while masking the inequities that exist for many individuals attempting to live fully as citizens. Paradoxically, the possibilities of citizenship depend upon such understandings as necessary precursors to engagements that may have profound sociopolitical effects. The possibilities of citizenship demand that we take care to understand as best we can how differences shape the degree to which we are able to engage as citizens in the world. They also entail a certain degree of attentiveness, a level of caring for self and others, for the world that evokes a need to act in ways that ameliorate the conditions of oppression. To further illustrate my belief that citizenship operates in education as (im)possibility, it is necessary, even crucial to uncover the deceptions of citizenship woven throughout liberal democracies, particularly as they advance citizenship as unproblematic and as a universal. Similarly, schools as discursive sites of citizenship propagate a particular conceptualization of citizenship that creates a precarious reality for teachers and students who are not all the same, but who find their differences disappearing in the face of "good" citizenship. Despite such deceptions, however, citizenship as a concept remains open enough to offer new possibilities for understanding what it means to be a citizen. The challenge is to find such openings in education and put them to work for the benefit of students and teachers.

The Deceptions of Citizenship

Because theories of liberal democracy embrace a universality of citizenship in relation to the rights and freedoms of individuals within a nation-state, there is an inherent assumption that these rights function to equalize individuals, that citizenship is full membership in a community whereby differences become irrelevant to individuals' status as citizens (Marshall, 1950). However, some degree of scepticism exists as to whether the "universality" of citizenship is indeed a reality. Taylor (1989) for example draws attention to the "failure of citizenship rights vested in liberal democratic institutions to meet the needs of women and racialized groups and the socially and economically marginalized (p.29)." Siim (2000) maintains that power differentials exist between women and men within current conceptions of citizenship. Voet (1998) expresses concern that because liberalism "already defines everyone as free citizens" it masks differentials in freedom between groups (p. 59) and Kymlicka (1995) wonders whether we can even talk about citizenship "in a society where rights are distributed on the basis of group membership (p. 174)." Each of these individuals stresses how liberal democratic citizenship has not lived up to its potential for universality despite divergent claims.

However, understandings of citizenship within liberal democracies continue to stubbornly profess universality simply because the state bestows certain rights on individuals. Such conjectures are troubling for they fail to recognize not only the complexities of citizenship, but also the inherent difficulties of political participation for individuals who occupy less privileged facets of society or who have historically been marginal to the state. Dillabough and Arnot (2000) draw attention to this marginality through their critique of the universal discourse of citizenship and its gendered construction of the rational citizen. They suggest that this construction was solidified in classical Greece when Aristotle conceived of the polis or public space as the sight of rational and reasoned dialogue. Only men, rational by nature, could engage in political activity while women were not to have a public or civic voice (Arnot, 2002; Lister, 1997a; Pateman, 1989; Stone, 1996). Instead, women were to care for the home, freeing men to engage in civic acts. While we are centuries removed from ancient Greece, citizenship has not necessarily transcended the exclusions that once shaped its very existence. Here, another rather dangerous assumption operates, one that believes that because rights are universally bestowed in liberal democratic nations, we are indeed living in a democracy. This assumption is challenged by Parker (2001) who suggests that democracy is not an achievement but something that must be continually aspired to. Despite these concerns he does not give up on notions of the democratic citizen as one who is "capable of democratic living, who want[s] it and who [is] determined to achieve it" (p. 1). However, Parker too makes an assumption that all individuals can work toward democratic ideals without really interrogating the construction of citizenship as a false universalism at the heart of "democracy" that prevents some citizens from fully participating in such a realization.

Schools as Discursive Spaces of Citizenship

Schools have a long and well-established relationship with citizenship and citizenship education, which as Cogan (2000) suggests

> ...has typically been an important goal in courses of study in history and civics in most nations and has, for the most part, focussed upon developing knowledge of how government and other institutions in any given state work, of the rights and duties of citizens with respect to the state and to the society as a whole and has been oriented largely towards the development of a sense of national identity. (p. 1)

Not only has citizenship been "an important" goal of many programs of study, the creation of "good citizens" has often been accorded prominence as the overarching aim of education. As institutions of liberal democratic education, schools then are caught up in the discursive production of "good" citizens, in which all individuals are thought equal, regardless of race, culture, class, gender, disability, or sexual orientation. Often, the terms "good" and "responsible" are used synonymously to designate certain desirable characteristics that individuals ought to engage in as citizens of a state or nation, or even of a classroom or school community. These terms serve as deceptive measures of equality when citizenship is constructed as universal and all students in a classroom are believed equally capable of becoming good or responsible citizens. Disparities in participation, particularly when political in nature, are thought to be the function of individual choice rather than inequity. Differences of class, ethnicity, gender, disability, sexual orientation, etc., are masked by the discourse of liberal democracy, which falsely promises that difference is rendered irrelevant to an individual's status as citizen and an individual's ability to engage as a citizen (Yuval-Davis,1997).

Joel Westheimer and Joseph Kahne (2004) argue that conceptions of "good citizenship" and conceptions of the good society are inextricably linked to democratic programs shaped by "ideologically conservative conception[s] of citizenship embedded in many current efforts at teaching for democracy" (p. 237). Thus, citizenship is less often constructed in terms of understanding social problems and improving society, or understanding how existing conditions of oppression inhibit the realization of democracy, and more often constructed in terms of acting responsibly and working within existing sociopolitical structures. Westheimer and Kahne (2004) refer to this type of citizenship education in schools as personal responsibility, whereby individuals do their part through such personal actions as recycling, voting, making charitable contributions, and obeying laws. In addition, participatory citizenship encourages students to understand how social and political organizations work by actively participating in them. This approach to citizenship might involve organizing a fundraiser, participating in youth parliament, or even campaigning for a political candidate. However, Westheimer and Kahne suggest, without attempting to undermine the value of each of these approaches, that they fail to acknowledge the causes of social inequities and as such, fail to really understand the roots of oppression. Participation without democratic enlightenment, argues Parker (2003), "may be worse than apathy" (p. xx). Thus, personal responsibility and participatory citizenship without a self-reflective and critical understanding of power and privilege may do more to sustain current inequities than to disrupt them. In addition, I would argue that these models of citizenship education do not account for the diverse contexts of students that may or may not inhibit their involvement in such endeavours. Students who are able to engage as participatory citizens are likely those who occupy more privileged social locations.

Similarly, the standardization of education fails to acknowledge the conditions of oppression at play in society, reinforcing a normalized vision of good citizenship, which constructs students as basically the same. The creation and implementation of standardized curriculum outcomes in social studies, uniform content, and common exams further reinforce the false universalism of citizenship embedded in education and promote an egalitarian conceptualization of education. It implies the existence of the "good" society, in that we are already all equal, and the need to preserve this society through educational practices. Vinson (2001, p. 64) argues however, that such standardization is a form of oppression as it "refuses to take seriously the notion and conditions of difference," reinforcing the inequalities that exist in broader society and in the world. Not only might this standardization be regarded as oppressive, it may also be understood as constructing a form of citizenship that is itself oppressive and oppressing.

A Differentiated Universalism

Ruth Lister (1997), a leading feminist scholar and political theorist has suggested that we need to move beyond the egalitarian discourse of citizenship, but not give up on the universalism that informs it. What she suggests is the necessary acknowledgment of how gender, culture, race, class, religion (and I would add, sexual orientation and disability) all come to bear on our constructions as citizens but that we must not abandon the potential for the universal "against which the denial of full and genuine citizenship to women and minority groups can be measured and claims for inclusion can be directed" (p. 88). For Lister, this differentiated universalism requires a synthesis of the universal and the particular. Through such a synthesis a creative tension emerges between universalism and diversity, and we are better able to realize the possibilities of citizenship and its fluidity beyond the liberal democratic discourse that disguises difference. Like Lister, Minnich (1990) maintains that "equality need not mean sameness, but, rather, that equality protects our right to be different" (p. 70). Arnot and Dillabough (1999) also recognize the importance of bringing diversity into discussions of citizenship and suggest that we view democracy "as one of many local sites where political power is both exercised over, and expressed by, individuals who are positioned differently within the polity" (p. 176). Citizenship, to be antioppressive, must not only acknowledge difference, it must embrace diversity as an integral component of the way in which we construct and enact our own understandings of citizenship.

Social Studies and the Forces of Citizenship

Canadian social studies educator Alan Sears (1997) argues that citizenship is a contested concept; this contestation is not reflected in the normative liberal democratic understandings of citizenship embedded in most social studies curriculum (Stone, 1996). Instead, social studies curriculum accepts that democracy is a given and fails to reflect upon its own role in sustaining citizenship as falsely universal. Thus, social studies curriculum, with its central goal of citizenship education, must be implicated in promulgating the conditions of oppression that exist in our society. It first must be understood as existing within and being produced by traditions of knowledge that privilege certain groups while marginalizing and excluding others. It should also be understood as perpetuating citizenship as falsely universal through the content and knowledge that students learn, and in many educational contexts, through high-stakes testing and common exams. The rhetoric of standardization and testing rigor which permeates social studies discourse in many Canadian schools ultimately allows students and teachers to enact a citizenship that lacks deep and deliberative understanding insofar as classrooms become places to prepare for exams, focus on results, and uncritically accept that the objectives of citizenship can be measured on a standardized test.

I want to turn now to the voices and stories of five high school teachers teaching social studies in Alberta to illustrate the inherent tensions of citizenship education as it aspires to create "good" citizens. Through a series of conversations with each of these teachers over a five-month period, we came to understand citizenship education as filled with tensions and perplexing difficulties. While each teacher spoke about the possibilities of education for citizenship, they also came to understand the many difficulties in a subject that has historically constructed citizenship as universal, and which is now enveloped in a climate of high stakes, standardized testing. For these teachers, citizenship played out in the classroom in ways that contradicted what they imagined as the inherent possibilities of citizenship for social change and deep understanding. I will touch briefly on some of the impossibilities now and then contrast them with the possibilities of citizenship articulated by these teachers as they imagined what citizenship might be within and beyond the classroom.

The Impossibilities of Citizenship

The theme of "citizenship as consumption of information" emerged among the teachers in relation to the emphasis placed on information to be tested on the final (diploma) exam as opposed to information that would better help students to live in and understand their world. For example, one of the participants, Denis, found himself teaching to the test, caught up in the ever-present reality of diploma exams, student achievement, and teacher results. Another participant Lois, suggested that the way she gained her students' attention at the beginning of class was to tell them that two marks on the final (diploma) exam would be found in the topic of discussion for that day. In both Denis' and Lois' classrooms, citizenship became much more about the consumption of information, both sociocultural and curricular, rather than a sustained questioning or critique of the traditions of knowledge in social studies.

Because of this desire for performance on the diploma exam, these individuals found themselves performing choices as teachers, and ultimately as citizens "responsible" for the education of young people. There is nothing straightforward about these performances, no scripts to follow and no lines to be memorized. The most constant and unyielding aspect of such performances are the predictability of the exam and the knowledge that so much is at stake because of it, including the possibilities for meaningful and engaged citizenship. In many respects, the diploma exam constructs citizenship as an outcome-based performance that is measurable and graded. Returning for a moment to the notion of "responsible" citizenship, these teachers seemed caught between their responsibility to get students through the exam and their responsibility to liberate students from the constraints imposed by the exam.

Citizenship as playing the game was perhaps the most troubling construction revealed through this research project. Students learn to play a particular game in social studies, one that may require them to shut down their own need to question curriculum content and sidestep grey areas in classroom conversations. How students take up the concept of citizenship and construct themselves as citizens in social studies classes depends upon what they perceive as the game of social studies. If winning the game means passing the exam and the course, then students do what they think they have to do in order to succeed. And if winning the game means fitting into an existing system or structure, then students may not want to stand outside of or question this system, even if they do not see themselves reflected in it or are made marginal by it. In social studies classrooms, then, students come to be "good" citizens in so far as they are able to successfully play the game. Those who are perceived as weaker, as potentially failing the exam, are marginalized by teachers who seek to "unload" them in lower level classes. One of the participants, Carol, believed that in her school, the culture of standardized exams was reinforced through choices teachers made in an effort to play the results game. What this suggests is that "good" citizenship has little to do with meaningful engagement in the world outside of school and certainly has even less to do with understanding sociopolitical conditions of oppression and how they might inhibit the possibilities for full citizenship. A central irony emerges between the perceived ability differences amongst students that prevent them from participating "fully" in their learning environment and a belief that citizenship is still universal in education.

Citizenship as playing the game lends itself to an understanding of citizenship that is self-interested, individualistic, and disciplinary. As with many games, there are rules, there are winners, and there are losers; so too with this game will there be winners and losers, but it is the winners who will be held up as exemplars of "good citizenship" within the system. As long as standardized exams are justified as rigorous assessment tools and as important indicators of the success of Canadian education in relation to other systems around the world, students and teachers will likely continue to play the game of "good citizenship" in social studies classrooms.

Similarly, citizenship as the path of least resistance is highly individualistic and equally self-serving. One of the teachers in this study, Wayne, felt that as citizens we have a responsibility to speak up about injustices but that we often accept the status quo because it is the path that seems safest. Disparate voices may be quiet or are quieted in the midst of political debate because to do otherwise makes these voices vulnerable to criticism and sanction. Wayne wondered whether social studies created spaces for students to speak up in opposition to a dominant point of view perpetuated via curriculum content. For students, it is often safer to accept the knowledge that is disseminated to them in social studies classes rather than engaging in a critique or exploration of the complexity of the information they are presented. In the gaze of the diploma exam, students may be constructed as passive receptacles of information, learning what they have to do to get by and to get through (Couture, 2000). Teachers too may choose the path of least resistance in how they approach the dissemination of social studies content. Rather than critiquing curriculum with students or attempting to unpack the deep traditions of knowledge embedded in content, teachers may choose instead to present the content of social studies unproblematically and uncritically, avoiding potential conflict and anxiety.

The Possibilities of Citizenship

Despite the impossibilities of citizenship that these five teachers faced in their own practice, they refused to give up on what they perceived as the possibilities of citizenship for themselves and their students. Without exception, each teacher spoke about social studies as offering spaces for engaging students in meaningful learning.

They also saw the social studies curriculum, particularly the current events component, as a vehicle through which students might connect with the world beyond the classroom in genuine ways. Their articulations of citizenship as understanding creates opportunities for exposing the false universalism embedded in political discourse and the conditions of oppression that are disguised by this discourse. While each participant struggled in similar ways with her or his own understanding of citizenship, no one was willing to concede entirely to the curricular definition of citizenship. For me, this speaks to the persistent possibility of opening up understandings of citizenship in education, moving beyond the falsely universalistic principles upon which it is structured, freeing it from the confines of the curriculum and of public spaces by continually constructing citizenship as we live it in multiple and varied ways, in multiple and varied locations. For social studies teachers, the persistent possibility of opening up understandings of citizenship means that we do not have to accept the "universality" of citizenship. While this may seem in tension with the prescribed curriculum, it is a productive tension precisely because understanding remains open.

Reimagining the Possibilities of Citizenship

Chantal Mouffe (1992) writes "old versions of citizenship have become an obstacle to making democracy work [in] more genuinely inclusive way[s]" (p. 184). I would take her assertions a step further and suggest that such conceptualizations of citizenship prevent the full realization of democracy as they attempt to mask social and political inequities marked by individual and group differences. Old versions of citizenship fail to truly understand the conditions of oppression that operate within our society. Yet, as Lister (1997) reminds us, we should not give up on the universality of citizenship as something that we must continually strive for. This is, I believe, what the teachers in my study imagined and attempted to articulate as the possibilities of citizenship within and beyond schools, and this is, I believe, what contributes to the tensions of citizenship in education. Despite their own struggles in relation to the false universalism of citizenship, these teachers refused to give up on citizenship as a transformative potential. They refused to accept the final word of citizenship as already universal. Yet, a politics of (im)possible citizenship becomes tangled up in a curriculum that refuses to interrogate its own conditions of oppression, and in an educational structure that privileges standardization and high-stakes testing. Nina Eliasoph (2000, p. 4) wonders how "thoughtful, everyday, philosophical, moral and political conversations go underground" as children enter school and how we might raise good citizens in a bad state, that is, a state that continues to oppress and marginalize many of its citizens. While I do not agree that these types of conversation completely disappear in schools and in social studies classrooms as evidenced in my conversations with the five teachers, I would propose that one of the challenges before us is how, in the face of standardization, oppressive curriculum and constructions of citizenship that seem to support rather than subvert conditions of oppression, we realize the possibilities that still exist to move away from the discursive stubbornness of citizenship in education. Perhaps I have raised more questions than I have answered over the course of this chapter, but these questions present an opportunity to reengage with the concept of citizenship in education, and in particular reengage with how citizenship is constructed and how individuals are and might be constructed by citizenship as they live.

References

Arnot, M. (1997). 'Gendered citizenry': New feminist perspectives on education and citizenship. *British Educational Research Journal, 23*(3), 275-295.
Arnot, M. (2002). *Reproducing gender? Essays on educational theory and feminist politics.* London: Routledge.
Arnot, M. & Dillabough, J. (1999). Feminist politics and democratic values in education. *Curriculum Inquiry, 29*(2), 159-189.
Cogan, J. J. & Derricott, R. (Eds.) (2000). *Citizenship for the 21st century: An international perspective on education.* London: Kogan Page.
Couture, J. C. (2000). *The gift of failure.* Unpublished doctoral dissertation. Edmonton: University of Alberta.
Dillabough, J. & Arnot, M. (Eds.) (2000). *Challenging democracy: International perspectives on gender, education and citizenship.* London: Routledge Falmer.
Eliasoph, N. (2000). Immeasurable pleasure and meaningful imperfection: Raising good citizens in a bad state. *Political Communication, 17*(1), 1-6.
Kymlicka, W. (1995). *Multicultural citizenship: A liberal theory of minority rights.* Oxford: Clarendon Press.
Lister, R. (1997a). *Citizenship: Feminist perspectives.* New York: New York University Press.
Lister, R. (1997b). Dialectics of citizenship. *Hypatia, 12*(4), 1-13.
Marshall, T. H. (1950). *Citizenship and social class.* Cambridge: Cambridge University Press.
Minnich, E. (1990). *Transforming knowledge.* Philadelphia: Temple University Press.
Mouffe, C. (1992). Feminism, citizenship and radical democratic politics, in J. Butler and J.W. Scott (Eds.), *Feminists theorize the political,* pp. 369-384. New York: Routledge.
Parker, W. C. (2001). Toward enlightened political engagement. In W.B. Stanley (Ed.), *Critical issues in social studies research for the 21st century,* pp. 97-118. Greenwich, CT: Information Age Publishing.
Parker, W.C. (2003). *Teaching democracy: Unity and diversity in public life.* New York: Teachers College Press.
Pateman, C. (1989). *The disorder of women.* Stanford, CA: Stanford University Press.
Sears, A. (1997). Social studies in Canada, in I. Wright & A. Sears (Eds.), *Trends and issues in Canadian social studies,* pp. 18-38. Vancouver: Pacific Educational Press.
Siim, B. (2000). *Gender and citizenship: Politics and agency in France, Britain and Denmark.* Cambridge: Cambridge University Press.
Stone, L. (1996). Feminist political theory: Contributions to a conception of citizenship. *Theory and research in social education, 24*(1), 36-53.
Taylor, D. (1989). Citizenship and social policy. *Critical social policy, 26*(1), 19-31.

Vinson, K. (2001). Oppression, anti-oppression, and citizenship education, in E. W. Ross (Ed.), *The social studies curriculum: Purposes, problems, and possibilities (revised edition)*, pp. 57–84. New York: State University of New York Press.

Voet, R. (1998). *Feminism and citizenship*. London: Sage Publications.

Westheimer, J. & Kahne, J. (2004). What kind of citizen? The politics of educating for democracy. *American Educational Research Journal*, 41(2), 237–269.

Yuval-Davis, N. (1997). Women, citizenship and difference. *Feminist Review*, 57(1), 4–27.

Hans Smits

"WEAK ONTOLOGY" AS A WAY OF REENCHANTING CITIZENSHIP IN THE SOCIAL STUDIES
A Memo with Some Random Notes

A "Memo" with Random Notes

A large part of learning takes place in the experience of the concrete.
(MARTHA NUSSBAUM, 1990)

The concepts in which thinking is formulated stand silhouetted like dark shadows on a wall. (H. G. GADAMER, 1998)

The ensuing "memo" is an attempt to put into play some questions about how we might talk about curriculum, especially in relation to the difficulties related to the subject of social studies and the idea of citizenship. I will narrate this as a precarious task at best, one fraught, as Judith Butler (2004) recently argued, with issues of the veracity of our representations and the question of where our responsibilities as curriculum people lie.

My memo with random notes is intended to foreground the partiality of the task. Creating a memo—engaging in memory—is also an active process not just of recollection, but in Ricoeur's terms, an act of *mimesis,* of putting into play various sources of experience and interpretation, through the detours required for understanding. This is not to simply say what one already knows, but facing up to the necessity of the hermeneutic task; as Ricoeur notes, a process that understanding requires "one to go by the detour of others, always valuing the detour of critique" (1998, 33).

"Random" is perhaps not the right word to describe the following set of notes, but I use the term to subvert my own desire to state authoritatively what social studies and citizenship ought to be. The notion of randomness as I use it is to admit to the ambiguity of the task that we face as teachers and researchers in the field of curriculum. Two common threads in the discussion, however, perhaps belie randomness: a ruing of "disenchantment," and a claim for "felicitous weak ontology" (Bennet, 2001).

Both the idea of the reenchantment of the world and the attempt to think of citizenship through the lens of a "weak ontology" represent efforts to think ethically and affirmatively beyond the dangers of impassivity and nihilism inherent in some forms of postmodern thought, but without succumbing to metaphysical certainty. The assertion of a "weak ontology" signals an attempt to rethink the importance of certain "attachments" required for ethical life. As Jane Bennett writes in *The Enchantment of Modern Life,* enchantment has to be seen as an "existential reality," as something that, while recognizing despair, can coexist with it, acknowledging "a stubborn attachment to life" (Bennet, 2001, 159–60).

Stephen White looks for ways that we can think differently about the human subject that we have inherited from modernist and humanist traditions of sovereign individualism, and latterly, the postmodern subject of indefinite identity and attachment. Both notions of the citizen, White argues, can be caught with the metaphor, the "Teflon subject," an idea of the self that is set free from any attachments or commitments, a "disengaged self"(White, 2000, 10). In its place, White advocates for a "stickier" view of the subject, "a deep reconceptualization of human being in relation to its world" and one who can, albeit in finite ways, account and support a conception and practice of citizenship without appeal to transcendent categories, but nonetheless carry ethical purpose (White, 2000, 9–10). Like Bennett, White appeals to certain kinds of "existential realities" of human life which can sustain "an adequately reflective ethical and political life"(8). I provisionally introduce these ideas as possible threads, which, if not firmly avoiding randomness, perhaps provisionally baste together my fragmentary notes. My notes represent an effort to attune to the places of ambiguity and struggle through and with difficult questions that face us as educational and curriculum practitioners—to struggle interpretively with some of those "dark shadows on a wall" described by Gadamer.

Layers of Difficulty in Relating Social Studies and Citizenship

The social studies has, like schooling more generally, suffered from conflicting and contesting aims (Stanely, 2001). The difficulty has perhaps intensified with the heightened awareness of the tension between asserting a common aim for the purposes and goals of social studies and the desire to acknowledge and represent difference, particularly cultural difference. As George H. Richardson has thoughtfully pointed out in his study of identity in the social studies curriculum, current attempts at defining social studies in terms of an overarching view of identity and common purposes for social studies remain in tension with the pull to adequately take up the realities of cultural difference (Richardson, 2002).

A notion of citizenship oriented by some belief in national identity, for example, or in the notion of the sovereign individual, is difficult to sustain in a world where the markers of identity have shifted. In part that requires challenging some of the forms of thought that have framed our work in social studies. Here I may take a cue from the work of writers such as Stephen Toulmin who identify modernism with abstracted, generalized, and decontextualized forms of knowledge (Toulmin, 1990). Thus although the social studies are arguably about social life, in general students may find little of themselves in it; the concept of citizenship is an abstract one, rather than living at the level of practice, which as Toulmin argues, has been neglected in modernist conception of the relation between thought and action (Toulmin, 1990).

Another layer of difficulty has to do with understanding the idea of citizenship in itself. As Eamonn Callan has written, it is not at all clear how citizenship is understood when used in the context of curricular aims (Callan, 1997). And when a conception of citizenship is unclear, there is also a kind of double danger: that ideological beliefs make their way into the curriculum, or as is often the case, while enshrined as a goal of the social studies, largely ignored. Perhaps in general this can be summed up by saying that it is not often clear whether citizenship refers to an idea or a practice.

The third layer of difficulty concerns the question of responsibility held by curriculum, that is, in a broad sense, what curriculum has to offer young people. In part, this question calls on Hannah Arendt's notion of belatedness: that education always lives between the past and future, and carries the ambivalent responsibility to bring children into a world that already exists, but also to prepare them to renew that world: citizenship cannot be simply understood as a preparation for the future, nor simply captured within the present (Arendt, 1993). As Ricoeur has written, this suggests a fundamental problem for public education, "the problem of democracy: how to educate citizens in critical adherence when as citizens they are never in the position of engendering the political sphere starting from themselves?" (Ricoeur, 1998, 102).

The difficulty revolves then, around the notion of citizenship as something for which one is prepared, and as preparation for a certain kind of practice, however tenuously that lives between past and future. But asked in that way, it refers to something critical about the nature of knowing and learning, for example, in Francesco Varela's terms, the differences and relations between "knowing-how" and "knowing-what"(Varela, 1999). Varela's work, as that of other "constructivist" thinkers would caution us that strong conceptions of something can never totally constitute adequately, learning. While we may hold strong convictions about citizenship, often those are either belied by teaching practices, or not addressed in terms of more active, practice-oriented ways of learning (Smits, 2001).

The Challenge of Immediacy in the Historical Moment

Arendt's notion about belatedness poses a challenge for citizenship in the social studies—and hence the question about how we both protect and prepare children for the world they are to inherit. The aim of citizenship in the social studies lives uneasily in this space. It may even succumb to what may be called the trope of crisis, cataclysm, or even apocalypse. Although not in imminent danger or upheaval, we may feel threatened by certain events or conditions that nonetheless make us feel anxious, spilling over into our everyday consciousness. In a commentary on the aftermath of September 11, 2001, Robert Bellah quotes the poet W.H. Auden's depiction of the mood on the eve of World War II as expression of this kind of anxiety:

> Waves of anger and fear
> Circulate over the bright
> And darkened lands of the earth,
> Obsessing our private lives (Auden in Bellah, 2002).

The moment we live in at the very present may or may not be as immediately calamitous as the impending war about which Auden expressed "anger and fear." But our lives too, are fraught with ambiguous events and looming uncertainties. "Obsessing our private lives" are events perhaps both beyond our reach, but nevertheless threatening. It always seems that it is our own historical moment that certain choices and dilemmas seem enlarged on the canvas representing our daily lives. There is immediacy to these events, however difficult to comprehend or fully describe, that makes it seem that the particular moment is unique and new. Another way to describe this problem is one of the relationship between memory and what memories ought to count, against the broader canvas of history. As we see in some current debates about whose stories ought to be represented in the social studies—what memories ought to be privileged or not—there is no shortage of memory, but nonetheless there may well be an absence of history (Huyssens, 2003).

I thought more about historical amnesia after reading Iain Pears' novel, *The Dream of Scipio* (Pears, 2002). The stories that Pears relates occur over three different periods of history, but all in the same place, a region in Provence in France: the fifth century, during the waning days of the Roman Empire; the fourteenth, at the apex of the black plague; and the twentieth, just before and during the Second World War. A major subtext in all three stories is the rise of antisemitism, set into motion within particular historical contexts: a belated attempt to assert Roman (and Catholic) sovereignty through targeting certain minorities, particularly Jews; the attempt to assign blame for the outbreak of the plague; and the persecution of Jews in occupied countries such as France as a way to appease German conquest.

Pears' novel acts as a reminder that what often feels immediate is not simply a repetition as Marx wrote of history, and not just an epiphenomenon to underlying forces of history, but nonetheless a kind of backdrop to what we experience as immediate. Pears' stories illustrate the idea of human action to which Arendt assigned narrative as its form of expression:

The chief characteristic of this specifically human life, whose appearance and disappearance constitute worldly events, is that it is always full of events which ultimately can be told as a story, establish a biography; it is of this life, *bios* as distinguished from mere *zoe*, that Aristotle said that it "somehow is a kind of praxis" (Arendt in Kristeva, 2001, p. 70).

Part of the question then about citizenship and social studies is how we understand such stories; how we give life to human action in the responsibility to help our students understand themselves in relation to their world. Citizenship, in the sense that Arendt gives to action, is not simply a reaction to the immediate, although it lives in the immediate. Hence, what may be at question here is specifically a form of practice, one that carries curricular and pedagogic imperatives to help weave memories into history.

As Georgia Warnke notes, "our historical situatedness does not only limit what we can know with certainty; it can also teach us how to remember and integrate what we must not forget" (Warnke, 2002, 41). Citizenship is not only something that lives in the present, is not just about the reaction to the immediacy of crises, but is something also embedded in time. And it is something that requires narration to show both the complexity of the immediate moment and how that moment is already deeply embedded in human time.

Ambivalence and Fragility in the Historical Moment

Perhaps only a novelist can capture fully the fragility and ambivalence of human action within the historical moment. Pears' novel, *The Dream of Scipio,* as described above is an example of both the ambivalence and fragility of the particular moments in which we are pushed to make sometimes difficult choices, exercise loyalty, or even just more prosaically, decide how we go on with our daily lives and responsibilities. In one of the stories, set in France in the Second World War, Julien, a would-be writer and academic, must decide between his love and loyalty for a woman of Jewish origin, his abhorrence of the German occupation, and protecting the identities of alleged members of the resistance. In the end, he accedes to the demands of the local administrator, Marcel, making a decision that is simply disastrous and tragic, "crushed by the words, all the arguments he might have summoned, all the reasoning like so much dust before the enormity of what Marcel had done"(Pears, 2002, 335).

The philosopher Martha Nussbaum has written extensively about how the abstract and objective rules for conduct and decision making can never fully account for the moment of decision making—that while there may indeed be a ground for our actions and decisions, how those are lived out, in moments of practical reasoning are always fragile and contingent, but nonetheless marked by necessity and the need to take responsibility (Nussbaum, 1986, 31–32). At one level, it is easy to condemn Julien in Pears' story above; on the other hand, as Nussbaum suggests, some stories also draw us back into the "depths of the particular" details of human action (69).

I again turn to a novel to illustrate Nussbaum's advice to consider the "depths of the particular" and as well, the fragility of the moment of action. The first part of Ian McEwan's *Atonement* (McEwan, 2001) occurs on one day, and concerns a young girl's fateful observation of an event that in her imagination and retelling dooms the fate of a young man, Robbie Turner. The story cuts across the interstices of particular historical events, social class, sexuality, time, and place. Robbie is convicted of a crime he did not commit, loses, in a sense everything, and ends up as a wounded enlisted man in Word War II. And the girl, Briony must live with the consequences of having narrated a pernicious tale. At one level, the novel works as a heart-breaking romance; at another, it raises questions about the adequacy of our accounts of the particular and what underlies our decisions. The difficulty and ambiguity of narration is perhaps caught by Robbie's injunction later in the story, when Briony is urged to make up for her "monstrous" deed:

> Then you'll write to me in much greater detail. In this letter you will put absolutely everything you think is relevant. Everything that led up to you saying you saw me by the lake. And why, even though you were uncertain, you stuck to your story in the months leading up to my trial. If there were pressures on you, from the police or your parents, I want to know. Have you got that? It needs to be a long letter. (p. 345)

In telling this story, McEwan turns his reflection on the writer's inability to atone for the imaginative reconstruction of events—we will never know "what *really* happened" but nonetheless one can and must attempt at atonement (371). McEwan helps us see that both moments of action, and the attempt to narrate them are fraught with difficulty, partiality—and as Ricoeur also suggests—motivation, intention, and subjectivity (Van den Hengel, 2002). So, I wonder when I look at the social studies curriculum, do we engage students in that precarious practice of not only recreating imaginative representations of history and memory, but also subject such narratives to the truth of practice?

Locating Citizenship in Students' Experiences of Teaching and Learning

Following this last question, I want to briefly refer to an exploratory study based on an inquiry into junior and senior high school students' experiences of teaching and learning (ATA, 2003). The study emphasized the *lived experiences of students,* focusing on their everyday experiences in classrooms. The experiences students related spoke to the common ways in which humans encounter and live in the world, for example, how we experience our bodies, how we inhabit space, how we discover and know ourselves as active meaning-making beings, and how all such experiences have a temporal quality.

As Merleau-Ponty has written, bodily experience is central to our experience in the world; as he noted evocatively, "Our own body is in the world as the heart is in the organism; it keeps the visible spectacle constantly alive, it breathes life into it and sustains it inwardly, and with it forms a system"(cited in Moran, 2000, 403). Bodies, in this sense, are where the world lives, where learning happens. From the perspective of recent work in the area of cognition, "embodiment" refers more concretely to the ways in which learners are fully engaged in creating meaning and action in actual situations (Varela, 1999).

Students' discussions about embodied experience illustrated some important aspects of learning. One is that as bodies, students as learners are not just passive objects: we are already part of the world as "whole" beings: physically, emotionally, and cognitively. It was not surprising to hear in students' voices what we as adults also experience: hunger, fatigue, and the effects of lack of sleep, illness, and various emotional states of mind. Plus, students provided a sense of embodiment as desire to be active in learning, that learning is about bringing the world and knowledge into being, what some writers refer to as the experience of *enactment* (Varela, 1993).

For the students with whom I talked, then, learning is a physical and emotional experience as well as a cognitive one. When learning happens, it is experienced as something that is pleasurable, that makes one feel that something important is happening. There was a strong sense in the students' words about the importance of learning that included the opportunities for application: that learning is not just learning *about,* about also learning to *do,* to create something new (Delors, et al, 1996).

Many of the students expressed the importance of having a sense of *agency* in learning. This may also be expressed as experiencing oneself more fully as a *capable* person. Ricoeur suggests in his discussion of becoming a self that there is a need to feel like someone who is capable, who can experience the esteem of being a person who is capable of understanding and doing (Ricoeur, 1992). The question about the capable person, he emphasizes, is "determining *who* can speak, *who* can act, *who* can recount, *who* can impute actions to himself or herself?"(Ricoeur, 1998, 89). Part of learning, in this sense, is to begin to develop a sense of the "who" of being a learner. To be capable is not merely to be able to function well in a technical sense or in the sense of exercising a skill. To feel capable as a learner refers much more to a holistic sense of being able to fully participate in an activity and feel that it relates in a broader sense to one's self as a person. This again speaks to the embodied quality of learning, that learning is part of who I *am* as a person (Varela, 1993, 149).

The discussion of embodiment as a key experience of learning caused me to reflect further about both the nature of social studies and what citizenship might mean in terms of the lived experiences of school and learning. Physical and emotional qualities of learning spoke to certain qualities of engagement, participation, and attachment in the world. Students expressed a strong desire to experience what hermeneutic scholars write about in philosophical terms . . . that learning is not simply abstract but requires active participation and application (Varela, 1999) and, as Varela notes, a "bringing forth" of meaning from a background of different experiences and resources (Varela, 1993, 149). When learning was not experienced as such, students expressed very much a *disenchantment* with their school experiences.

Terms of Disenchantment

The idea of disenchantment has been an important one, especially in late twentieth-century social theory and philosophy, and is often associated with what Charles Taylor has called the "malaise of modernity," which particularly identifies the over-instrumentalized qualities of life in institutions as both a root cause and effect (Taylor, 1991; Borgmann, 1992). And the more recent postmodern literature has identified the disenchantment with overly rationalized, Cartesian-based approaches to knowledge and learning (Toulmin, 1990, 2001). Such critiques echo my concerns about the disembodied qualities learning that students experience in their lives, where the absence of practice is felt as an absence of learning, and as Bennet suggests, an absence of meaningful attachment and vitality (Bennet, 2001, 4).

Disenchantment is a realization that increased technical mastery of our work and world, and the world of abstracted knowing, does not resolve questions of meaning and purpose, as Max Weber wrote (Weber, 1946, 139). Yet we may cling to the belief that technical solutions and procedures may hold those broader questions at bay, if not render them totally irrelevant, just as in education, we may put great stock in the results of standardized testing in the absence of deeper questions of meaning and purpose.

Discussions of social studies curriculum and how to incorporate citizenship are not immune to disenchantment. Underlying the social studies remains the idea that rationality, programs, and the right knowledge will win the day. Hence, social studies may fall into a kind of disenchantment—that is to say, both disillusionment with its promise to resolve enduring problems of practice and meaning and another promotion of the right methods and approaches, which fails to engender meaningful attachment.

However, the quest for certainty, as John Dewey discussed in his work, may only lead away from enchantment, away from encounters with the particular, with possibilities that do not yet exist, and "the failure to recognize that human experience is the situated awareness within which feeling occurs and within which problems are felt, articulated, and resolved"(cited in Hickman, 1998, xx). In Dewey's terms, seeing citizenship, for example, as an end of the social studies, only serves, in the argument I am making, to disenchant. As he wrote, "When ends are regarded as literally ends to action rather than as directive stimuli to present choice they are frozen and isolated" (cited in Archambault, 1974, 73). This is not to argue that thinking about social studies and citizenship is aimless or can be left to haphazard choice but it is to think about the nature of purposes in social studies and how it takes up the education of the young. Dewey, for one (72), and more recently Nel Noddings (Noddings, 2003), argued for a way that we might begin to think differently about the aims and purposes of curriculum, illustrating the importance of direction and purpose, but emphasizing how the educational task is embedded in the activity, not just the aim.

"Felicitous Weak Ontology" as a Way to Begin Talking about Citizenship and Social Studies

Stephen White discusses the possibilities for ethical and political action which do not rest on the "modernist" ideal of the sovereign, disengaged subject, nor on the decentered, fractured postmodern one. He wants to identify a way that one might talk about subjectivity and action that does not depend on more traditional ontological concepts. Strong ontologies, as he calls those, "carry an underlying assumption of certainty that guides the whole problem of moving from the ontological level to the moral-political"(White, 2000, 7).

White argues, however, that such ontologies fail to deal with ambiguity, uncertainty, and contingency, and the kinds of questions of difference and power that postmodern and poststructural thinkers have brought to fore in recent times. I think this is the argument that I have been making as well—randomly—about social studies and citizenship: that asserting strong ontologies—e.g. as to what constitutes human nature, political identity, historical knowledge, and the correct concepts for understanding—have not helped us to figure out a more enchanted form of social studies and a form of citizenship that may live as a practice and meaningful learning experience for students.

Nonetheless—and I would agree with this—White argues that there has to be something that allows for a "stickier" subject, one who could take up ethical responsibilities and live out meaningful attachments. White's defense of a weak ontology acknowledges on the one hand the contestability of all notions of the self, other and world, but on the other hand that they are necessary for thinking about possibilities for ethical and political action (White, 2000, 9).

White articulates further the possibilities inherent in certain "existential realities"—natality, sources of the self, language, and finitude—which can be said to be constitutively universal, yet at the same time, flexible, open, and subject to interpretation and contingency, and critically, what it means to be "a certain sort of creature"(9). Such existential realities provide a language in which we might begin to articulate a sense of what social studies might do as a subject in schools. Weak ontology provides a way to think about citizenship that takes up Arendt's difficulty of living between past and future and begins to understand it as something embedded in language and traditions but also as something that may be understood as a practice of learning. White explains how a weak ontology lives in a circuitous and interactive relationship among judgments and norms in specific contexts of action, "we" claims, and narratives which relate to self and other.

Reenchanting the Social Studies and Citizenship

The notes in this memo include some reservations about asserting strong foundations of curriculum within the recognition of the difficulties inherent in social studies and the goal of citizenship. The immediacy of the historical moment, as I tried to argue earlier, can foster despair and a certain kind of inertia, if not outright hopelessness. But moments of immediacy are also where experience lives, as I tried to illustrate through a discussion of students' experiences of learning. Bennett captures well my own conflicted feelings about the possibilities of citizenship, and a social studies than can help students experience a "reenchantment" of the world, asking how it is possible to write of enchantment in a world that frequently offers little cause for it (Bennet, 2001, 159–60).

Bennett's concern involves the question of what can allow for stronger ethical life—in her terms, what may engender "normative courage." Here she turns to White's "felicitous weak ontology" as providing a ground, in a sense, for action: that attending to the "fundamental character of human being and the world" through attunement to the existential qualities of language, finitude, sources, and natality, through stories which can appeal to experience and "assent wholeheartedly to life"(159–60).

Her own examples are provocative: she writes of the materiality of both human and interspecies relationships, the possibilities in forms of reason and mathematics, and the imaginative readings and narratives of experience that may open possibilities for thinking other than what is. My brief examples of students' experiences serve as a reminder that where learning "works" for students is not in the abstract, and not in some prefigured moment of achievement of understanding but very much in experience, in moments when forms of attachment and forms of imagination may come together with a sense of oneself as a person.

To take up the task of enchanting the social studies is to admit to what Butler has termed precariousness, but a precariousness that doesn't absolve us of responsibility; indeed it returns us to what is "other"—other in not just a sociological sense, but also other in ourselves, in what might be, and in other ways of understanding and representation (Butler, 2004). There are resources we can begin to draw on that take up the challenge of reenchanting the world, through the kinds of existential realities identified as both the ground and source of understanding and ethical action (Parker, 2001). For example, although we may be ambivalent or critical of White's "Teflon" self, we nonetheless ought to take seriously the idea of how one narrates a life, or as Charles Taylor has expressed it, what allows for a more sustainable authenticity (Taylor, 1991).

The philosopher Martha Nussbaum, in recognizing the poverty of certain educational narratives, wants to pull us back into the ways that acknowledge the importance of education in what she calls "cultivating humanity:" that a "liberal" form of education must allow for a "critical examination of oneself and one's traditions" but also to see themselves not just citizens in a local sense, but as citizens bound to other human beings by "ties of recognition and concern,"(Nussbaum, 1997) echoing Bennett's emphasis on attachment and enchantment.

As she and other writers have emphasized, this requires the work of narrative imagination—which has particular import for ethical ways of being. In the words of the moral philosopher Alisdair MacIntyre, "deprive children of stories and you leave them unscripted, anxious stutterers in their actions as in their words"(MacIntyre, 1984, 216). And such stories perhaps require some reference to something greater than just the self or oneself—becoming a self, and individual requires something beyond the self in order to warrant ethical ways of being and understanding (Seligman, 2000).

My "memo" and its set of random notes is, of course, highly incomplete. But what I have tried to do is create a reminder to those of us who work in curriculum—social studies in particular—to ask what might enchant our young people, that is what can help them "sing together" as the word *enchant* suggests, in a world that offers little security or certainty yet cries out for responsibility and attachment.

References

Arendt, H. (1993). *Between past and future: Eight exercises in political thought*. New York: Penguin Books.

Arnswald, U. (2002). On the certainty of uncertainty: language games and forms of life in Gadamer and Wittgenstein. In J. Malpas, U. Arnswald, & J. Kertscher (Eds.), *Gadamer's century. Essays in honor of Hans-Georg Gadamer* (pp. 25–44). Cambridge, MA: MIT Press.

Bellah, R. (2002). Seventy-five years. *The South Atlantic Quarterly 10 (2)*, 253–265.

Bennett, J. (2001). *The enchantment of modern life. Attachments, crossings, and ethics.* Princeton and Oxford: Princeton University Press.

Borgmann, A. (1992). *Crossing the postmodern divide*. Chicago: University of Chicago Press

Butler, J. (2004). *Precarious life. The powers of mourning and violence*. London and New York: Verso.

Callan, E. (1997). *Creating Citizens*. Oxford and New York: Oxford University Press.

Delors, J., et.al. (1996). *Learning. The treasure within*. Report to UNESCO of the International Commission on Education for the Twenty-first Century. UNESCO Publishing.

Dewey, J. (1922/1974). The nature of aims. In Archambault, R. (Ed.), *John Dewey on education. Selected writings*. Chicago and London: University of Chicago Press.

Gadamer, H.G. Reflections on my philosophical journey/ Hickman, L. (1998). Introduction. In L. Hickman (Ed.), *Reading Dewey. Interpretations for a postmodern generation* (pp. ix–xvii). Bloomington: Indiana University Press.

Huyssens, A. (2003). *Present pasts: Urban palimpsets and the politics of memory*. Stanford, CA: Stanford University Press.

Kristeva, J. (2001). *Hannah Arendt: Life is a narrative*. Toronto: University of Toronto Press.

MacIntyre, A. (1984). *After virtue. A study in moral theory*. Notre Dame, IN: University of Notre Dame Press.

McEwan, I. (2001). *Atonement*. Toronto: Vintage Canada.

Moran, D. (2000). *Introduction to phenomenology*. London and New York: Routledge.

Noddings, N. (2003). *Happiness and education*. Cambridge and New York: Cambridge University Press.

Nussbaum, M. (1986). The fragility of goodness. Luck and ethics in Greek tragedy and philosophy. Cambridge, MA: Cambridge University Press.

Nussbaum, M. (1990). *Love's knowledge: Essays in philosophy and literature*. New York: Oxford University Press.

Nussbaum, M. (1997). *Cultivating humanity. A classical defense of reform in liberal education*. Cambridge, MA, and London: Harvard University Press.

Parker, W. (2001). Toward enlightened political engagement. In Stanley, W. (Ed.), *Critical issues in social studies research for the 21st century* (pp. 97-118). Greenwich, CT: Information Age Publishing.

Pears, I. (2002). *The dream of Scipio*. Toronto: Alfred A. Knopf Canada.

Richardson, G. (2002). *The death of the good Canadian: Teachers, national identities, and the social studies curriculum*. New York: Peter Lang.

Ricoeur, P. (1992). *Oneself as another*. Chicago: University of Chicago Press.

Ricoeur. P. (1998). *Critique and conviction. Conversations with Francois Azouvi and Marc de Launay*. (K. Blamey, Trans.). New York: Columbia University Press.

Seligman, A. (2000). *Modernity's wager. Authority, the self, and transcendence*. Princeton, NJ, and Oxford: Princeton University Press.

Smits, H. (2001). Evaluation Study of the Teachers' Parliamentary Institute: Exploring the Impact of Participation in the Teachers' Institute and on the Understanding of Curriculum, Pedagogy and Citizenship Education. Report prepared to the Teacher Advisory Committee, Teachers' Institute on Canadian Parliamentary Democracy. Ottawa.

Stanley, W. (2001). Social studies:Problems and possibilities. In Stanley, W. (Ed.), *Critical issues in social studies research for the 21st century* (pp. 1-14). Greenwich, CT.: Information Age Publishing.

Taylor, C. (1991). *The malaise of modernity*. Toronto: Anansi.

The Alberta Teachers' Association. (2003). *Trying to teach, trying to learn: listening to students*. Edmonton: The Alberta Teachers' Association.

Toulmin, S. (2001). *Return to reason*. Cambridge, MA, and London: Harvard University Press.

Toulmin, S. (1990). *Cosmopolis. The hidden agenda of modernity*. Chicago: University of Chicago Press.

Van den Hengel, J. W. (2002). Can there be a science of action? In R. Cohen & J. Marsh (Eds.), *Ricoeur as another: The ethics of subjectivity* (pp. 71-92). Albany: State University of New York Press.

Varela, F. (1999). *Ethical know-how. Action, wisdom and cognition*. Stanford, CA: Stanford University Press.

Weber, M. (1946). *From Max Weber: Essays in sociology.* (H. H. Garth & C. Wright Mills, Trans.). New York: Oxford University Press.

White, S. (2000). *Sustaining affirmation. The strengths of weak ontology in political theory*. Princeton, NJ and Oxford: Princeton University Press.

Jyoti Mangat

WATCH THIS [WHITE] SPACE: CANADIAN STUDENTS INTERROGATING CITIZENSHIP AND IDENTITY

This chapter will discuss "whiteness" as it relates to notions of citizenship in contemporary, multicultural Canada with particular reference to a research project where high school students read the short story, "The Management of Grief" by Bharati Mukherjee (1988). This story, by an author who is highly critical of Canada's policy of official multiculturalism, is about the Air India bombing of 1985 and was read by 10 high school students who were then interviewed about their responses to the piece. Mukherjee (1997), in an interview, relates the following anecdote as an illustration of her critique of official multiculturalism in Canada:

> A terrorist bomb, planted in an Air-India jet on Canadian soil, blew up after leaving Montreal, killing 329 passengers, most of whom were Canadians of Indian origin. The Prime Minister of Canada at the time, Brian Mulroney, phoned the prime minister of India to offer Canada's condolences for India's loss. (paragraph 13)

The students, five of Indian-Canadian heritage and five of European-Canadian heritage, each had particularly strong responses to the portrayal of the single white character in a story populated largely by Indo-Canadian characters. One white student referred to this character, Judith Templeton, a government social worker assigned to act as a "cultural translator" between the stricken immigrant community and the government's social agencies, as "the icon of white." This chapter will discuss the students' responses to Judith and their perspectives on multiculturalism, identity, and citizenship in Canada.

The Text

Bharati Mukherjee's short story, "The Management of Grief" is "about the effects of the Air India disaster on Toronto's Indian community and specifically on the central character and narrator, Mrs. Shaila Bhave, who loses her husband and two sons in the crash" (Bowen, 1997, p. 48). The narrator appears to be coping well with the tragedy, and she is asked by a government social worker, Judith Templeton, "to help as an intermediary—or, in official Ontario Ministry of Citizenship* terms, a 'cultural interpreter'—between the bereaved immigrant communities and the social service agencies" (Bowen, 1997, p. 48). In her article, "Spaces of Translation: Bharati Mukherjee's 'The Management of Grief,'" Bowen tells us that:

> Judith is caught between worlds; she does not know how to translate the grief she shares with Shaila and the Indian community into cultural specifics that will be acceptable to both Indian and Western modes of thought. Shaila is initially caught, too, between different impulses coming from different cultural models, which she has internalized within her self. The question of how to effect moral agency while practicing the acceptance of difference is in both instances a tricky one. (1997, p. 49)

Both women occupy roles as translators and interpreters between two cultures, roles that are difficult and uncomfortable to occupy. Shaila, however, is the "dislocated mourner" (Bowen, 1997, p. 59) who must manage her own grief and that of others. Her sense of dislocation leads her on a journey that takes her from Canada to Ireland to India and back to Canada. Upon her return to Toronto, "Shaila is a figure for productive cultural hybridity. Standing on the translator's threshold, looking in both directions, she comes to possess the power to understand her liminality as itself a space for 'effective (moral) agency' (Mohanty 116)" (Bowen, 1997, p. 58).

This story was particularly appropriate for this study because of the very issues of cultural translation explored by Bowen. The story is about a very specific event in Canadian culture, but it may also be about an event specific *to* a Canadian culture. In "The Sorrow and the Terror: The Haunting Legacy of the Air India Tragedy" (1987), Blaise and Mukherjee tell us that they "saw it then, and see it now, as fundamentally an immigration tragedy with terrorist overtones" (p. ix).

The Research Participants

The ten students I interviewed were grade eleven and twelve students who attended two different high schools in a suburb of a western Canadian city. I sought five student volunteers of European heritage and five of Indian heritage and all of the students, with the exception of one European-Canadian male, were raised in

---

*Editor's note: Ontario is a province in Canada. The Provincial government, through its Ministry of Citizenship and Immigration, works to help newcomers settle in Ontario; immigration to Canada is under federal jurisdiction.

this community. Finding five students of East Indian background in this particular suburb was somewhat difficult since, as one of my interviewees commented, "[This place] is so not culturally diverse." However, with the help of teachers in the school district I was able to locate five volunteers. While these Indo-Canadian students shared much in common, they presented a number of interesting differences among themselves. They were all raised in this suburban community and were strong, highly social students; however, their backgrounds, all "Indian" to some extent, were diverse. The students of European background proved to be no less diverse than their Indo-Canadian counterparts. All of these students were also raised in the same community, with the exception of one, who lived in England between the ages of ten and sixteen. Again, these students were academically motivated and socially active in their schools. When I asked the student volunteers to tell me about their cultural backgrounds, none of the students of European heritage provided any information on religious affiliations, while the participants of Indian background did. The pseudonyms I have chosen for the students involved in this study reflect their real names to the extent that, especially for the Indo-Canadian students, I have attempted to maintain a connection to their specific cultural heritages. For example, Theresa's actual name reflects a Christian tradition rather than a Hindu tradition, and I have maintained that distinction here.

Students of Indian heritage:
Meena: 16, female, south Indian, Hindu
Theresa: 17, female, south Indian-Sri Lankan, Christian
Simi: 16, female, north Indian, Hindu
Raj: 18, male, Indo-Fijian, Hindu
Salim: 17, male, Indo-Ugandan, Muslim

Students of European heritage:
Joanne: 17, female, Scandinavian
Mary: 17, female, Scottish
Kristine: 16, female, Norwegian-Sioux
Alex: 17, male, Scandinavian
Colin: 17, male, British-Scandinavian

Culture and Multiculturalism in the 'Burbs

The suburb discussed in this study is a middle-class community of 50,000 and the population is made up overwhelmingly of white, professional, two-parent families. There is very little cultural or economic diversity, and the students I interviewed are aware that the community of their youth is quite unlike urban Canadian multicultural reality. In fact, Simi, a seventeen-year-old girl of Indian heritage, revealed that her older sister said that "going to university was a culture shock. Coming from here, you don't even think of yourself as Indian exactly. She said that she had never seen so many culturally different people in one room. She was shocked."

All of the students involved in my study offered similar insights into contemporary multiculturalism as they have seen it from their varying perspectives. Expressing a dissatisfaction with the reality of how multiculturalism has manifested itself in Canada, Simi revealed,

> They say that Canada is a multicultural society, but I think there's always gonna be that differentiation just because of the difference in looks. Canada is a country that is made up mostly of Caucasian people with fair skin. And I think that because we stand out so much I don't think we're going to see each other as 'Canadian.' Like when I walk down the street I can tell Italian people and Oriental people. I don't think oh, she's Canadian and she's Canadian. Like when you think about Europeans you think Caucasian, when you think of India you think Indians, you think of Africa you think of Black people, when you think of Canada you think of Caucasian people. When you think of North America that's what you think of. . . . And just because of that generalization we'll always stand out. Like when I think of Canada, myself, I think of Caucasian people.

The Indian students, despite having been faced with very little overt racism, agreed that they "haven't really experienced it hands on, but you can tell it's kind of on the back burner. It's there but no one says anything about it. No one treats you differently but they still make racist jokes and don't treat it as a serious matter."

This questioning of multiculturalism does not lie exclusively with the Indian students. Colin, a seventeen-year-old boy who told me that his family in England have been "fishermen since boats were invented," observed that,

> It seems like the problem with racism, you know, of multiculturalism failing, if you can say it has failed, is that there's this misunderstanding on both sides. And it's the lack of realizing that there's a misunderstanding that really creates the problem. And this [story] is sort of saying, look, there *is* a misunderstanding on both sides, face it.

Interestingly, the students involved in this study appear to be providing a perspective on an ongoing debate regarding Canadian multiculturalism. In her discussion of the writers Neil Bissoondath and Bharati Mukherjee, Margaret Cannon (1995) explains:

> While . . . the East Indian author Bharati Mukherjee [sees] Canada as an extremely racist society, Bissondath does not. . . . [Bissondath] states: 'I think every country is racist, unless it is a country that has only one race living in it. But Canada is less racist than most countries I can think of.' Bharati Mukherjee has often criticized Canada for being more racist than the United States, a position Bissoondath doesn't share. Bharati, he says, 'prefers the United States because there everything is up front. An American doesn't like you because of the colour of your skin, you will know it. And therefore Canada is a more racist country. I would much rather have a racist behave in

the Canadian way: smile and be polite . . . Canadians, even when they are racist, realize that it's not a nice thing to be.' (p. 250)

Both Mukherjee and Bissoondath came to Canada as immigrants from "hot, moist" (Mukherjee, 1985, p. 2) countries and both have been concerned with "the immigrant experience." However, since the Indian students I interviewed were the children of immigrants their relationship with Canada is necessarily different. Rather than being from "hot, moist" places like their parents, these young people are from a cold, dry land, and this does make a difference. These are young people who carry only vague, vacation memories of the climates of their parents and who have spent their childhoods with the real life memories of the smell of wet woolen scarves and varyingly successful attempts at ice-skating. This cold, dry prairie and those "hot, moist" places come together to create people who can "live on the hyphen" in surprising ways (quoted in Jones & Katel, July 10, 1995, p. 34).

Judith Templeton: "The Icon of White"

In "The Management of Grief" (Mukherjee, 1988), Judith Templeton is "an appointee of the provincial government," whose "mandate is bigger" than multiculturalism (p. 182). She arrives within days of the bombing to elicit the help of the narrator, Mrs. Shaila Bhave, in negotiating "the complications of culture, language, and customs" (Mukherjee, 1988, p. 183) associated with the tragedy. Judith fails to recognize the complexities within the Indian community in Toronto when she asks Shaila, a Hindu who has lost her husband and both sons in the bombing, to help two elderly Sikhs who have lost their adult sons in the same tragedy. The conflict and difference between Hindus and Sikhs, and the reality that Sikh terrorists planted the bomb, does not occur to Judith.

The students' responses to this character were quite clearly split along cultural lines. The Indo-Canadian students generally found Judith to be quite unsympathetic. Meena begins her comments sarcastically by saying:

> It seemed like she was, oh, 'the kind Canadian lady just trying to help out everyone.' She said all the . . . government wants to do is give these people money and they're too stubborn to accept it. I don't really agree with that very much because they're portraying her in a way like the government is just being so . . . kind of . . . being so *nice* to people but actually a lot of bigotry went along with this bombing. There was a lot of racism surrounding it . . . the way the Indian community was portrayed on the news and stuff wasn't very respectful.

This dissatisfaction with the character of the "kind Canadian lady" is evoked more emotionally with Theresa's comment that:

> It made me cry . . . it wasn't so much that it was about death . . . like that was sad, but this is going to sound strange . . . but you know [Judith] and how she's not necessarily racist, but she's so almost like, *ignorant* of culture and other peoples' culture . . . I

don't know, but I've never encountered racism directly, but you still kind of feel it. I don't know, but that just kind of hit.

Simi articulates a sense of ambivalence about the dissonance between the character's motives and the reality of her methods:

> [The story] made it seem like [Judith] was so good . . . made it seem like she was only trying to help, but she didn't really know anything about the situation. I didn't really know what to think of her.

The two Indo-Canadian boys, Raj and Salim, both echoed Meena and Simi with their observations:

> Raj states: At first I thought she was a nice person and just trying to help but I after reading what that old couple said . . . you don't want help from other people, you support your family . . . and how she kept persisting on them to do it [sign the power of attorney papers], I kind of started getting mad. Like, let them live their life the way they want. I don't think it's her place to go in to somebody and say you have to sign this to make your life better. How does she know it will make their life better and not worse?

> Salim comments: She tried to help them, but she didn't respect their need for closure, I guess, their own way to grieve. It was like she wanted to pay them off or something. . . . It's like she's *using* [Shaila's] nationality.

These students appear to be unwilling to excuse Judith's ignorance in the name of her benevolence despite the fact that all of them do acknowledge the difficulty of her task. In contrast, many of the Euro-Canadian students, even while recognizing her problematic status within the story, appeared to empathize with Judith's predicament. Joanne comments that:

> . . . She had good intentions I think . . . she was trying hard to do in her mind what would be the best for these people, but I think that the cultural differences were just so great that she didn't do a very good job of it at all. She insulted her [Shaila] when [Shaila] got out of the car and walked away and . . . she totally couldn't connect with the old lady and the old man. Like nothing she could say . . . like they were on two different wavelengths. Right, so, she was nice and . . . I kind of empathized with her. . . 'cause she tried so hard but she just couldn't connect at all.

And Alex, despite making the observation that Judith "totally represented cultural ignorance," went on to reveal a more personal response to Judith's actions:

> . . . I'm sure her heart was in the right place . . . what she was doing was trying to make these people's lives better, but she didn't ever try to step out her own little viewpoint and realize that there might be other viewpoints around . . . If you look at all the major colonial instances in history it's always been the colonizer coming in and saying 'these people are wrong. We have to educate them, we have to conform them to what's good.' She obviously was [doing] that but I don't think it was in-

tended . . . I can possibly understand how that would happen. I'm sure I've been guilty of it lots, too. I'm sure I offended hundreds of people in my old school because of my own viewpoints and how I don't really think about stuff.

Mary's response indicates a genuine confusion about Shaila's motives towards the end of the story. She says:

> I don't know why [Shaila] got so mad at her. [Judith] just seemed like she wanted to help. I can understand how she might have been pushing that old couple too hard, but I don't know why [Shaila] would have gotten out of the car. That lady was just trying to help.

Even Kristine and Colin, with their own interesting relationships with multiculturalism in Canada, responded with some measures of empathy toward Judith. Kristine, who revealed during our interview that she was half Sioux but 'passes' for white with her red hair and fair skin, said, "I can understand why, being white, she would want someone of that cultural background to help." Colin, who was dating an Indo-Canadian girl from a very culturally diverse area of a larger city, said: "I still see Judith as being representative of white people. And I think it's fair because she's really well meaning, but she's totally off base."

Most of the students of European heritage responded to the ambiguity of Judith's position within the story. They acknowledged that, despite her good intentions, her assumptions about Shaila and the Sikh couple were inappropriate.

> Joanne: She thought her way was the only way that was going to get things resolved, so she could have been more open to different possibilities. Obviously, if it wasn't working she should have tried different things.

> Alex: Like she didn't ever try to say, "Why don't these people want it? What's going on in their minds, what makes them click that way?" Instead, she was like, they're obviously wrong . . . She doesn't perceive the difference between Hindu and Sikh. She's like, "Here, you're that type. Talk to them for me because I'm not that type. I'm not your kind."

> Kristine: I thought it was a horrible thing to do . . . when [Judith] asks [Shaila] to help with the Sikh people, I thought that was really insensitive because she just lost her whole family in that plane crash. And she never even thought enough to realize that just because they're from the same country . . . there are different cultures. [Shaila] even told her, "They're not going to talk to me. I can't help them." And she couldn't understand that.

> Colin: I kind of have to see Judith as the icon of white . . . that's how white people treat everybody. And that's as good as at it gets. It gets a lot worse, but that's as *good* as it gets . . . and that's the way white Western people go somewhere to help out the "savages" and when they want to be *nice* about it then that's how they treat them. If they *don't* want to be nice about it, it's something else. They're very condescending,

as though getting along for thousands of years must have just been a fluke. So, if that's the intent, then it was a fair representation, if Judith was that.

Colin's somewhat cautious suggestion that perhaps Judith symbolically functions as the personification of Canadian official multiculturalism echoes Mukherjee's (1988) assertion that "Canada is a country officially hostile to the concept of assimilation... [it is] a comfortable but unwelcoming environment" (p. 1). In response to Judith, the official government representative, each participant in the study recognized, however cloaked by "niceness," the element of hypocrisy that Mukherjee clearly feels is an element of contemporary Canadian society.

Citizenship in Contemporary Canada

The insights offered by these high school students have powerful implications for notions of citizenship in contemporary Canada. These young Canadians expressed their skepticism towards multiculturalist policies in ways similar to such academics as Himani Bannerji (2000), who says that, "the discourse of multiculturalism, as distinct from its administrative, practical relations and forms of ruling, serves as a culmination for the ideological construction of 'Canada'" (p.96). By this, she means that those "on whose actual lives this ideology is evoked" are placed in a paradoxical situation:

> On the one hand, by our sheer presence we provide a central part of the distinct pluralist unity of Canadian nationhood; on the other hand, this centrality is dependent on our 'difference,' which denotes the power of definition that 'Canadians' have over 'others.' (p. 96)

The students in the study, regardless of ethnic origins, recognized the problematic nature of official multiculturalism in Canada and the issues related to citizenship. The question of who counts as "Canadian" brings us back to Mukherjee's anecdote regarding the Air-India bombing: 80% of the victims were Canadian citizens, yet it was imagined by the Canadian public to be India's tragedy. The RCMP's* handling of the criminal investigation has done little to dispel the suggestion that had the victims been white, matters may have been undertaken differently. Despite these disturbing realities, the conversations with these young Canadians suggest that perhaps, in their skepticism, they are able to see beyond the official story of multiculturalist discourse that has prevailed in Canada to date and are able to imagine a reality that moves forward in real and productive ways.

---

*Editor's note: The Royal Canadian Mounted Police (RCMP) is the federal police force of Canada.

References

Blaise, C. & Mukherjee, B. (1987). *The sorrow and the terror: The haunting legacy of the Air India tragedy*. Markham, Ontario: Viking Penguin.

Bowen, D. (1997). Spaces of translation: Bharati Mukherjee's "The management of grief." *ARIEL, 28*(3), 47-60.

Cannon, M. (1995). *The invisible empire: Racism in Canada*. Toronto, Ontario: Random House.

Chen, T. & Goudie, S. X. (1997). Holders of the word: An interview with Bharati Mukherjee. *Jouvert* [Online], *1*(1), 104 paragraphs. Available: *http://social.shass.ncsu.edu/jouvert/ 111/bharat.htm*.

Hancock, G. (1987). An interview with Bharati Mukherjee. *Canadian Fiction Magazine, 59*, 30-44.

Mukherjee, B. (1985). *Darkness*. Markham, Ontario: Penguin.

Mukherjee, B. (1988). The management of grief. In, *The middleman and other stories*, pp. 179-97. New York: Grove.

Mukherjee, B. (1997, January/February). American dreamer. *Mother Jones Magazine* [Online], 32 paragraphs. Available: *http://mojones.com/mother_jones/JF97/mukherjee.htm*.

Ingrid Johnston

DISLOCATING THE DOMINANT NARRATIVES OF CITIZENSHIP IN ENGLISH LANGUAGE ARTS

Literacy practices are inextricably linked with notions of citizenship, society, and the ways we live with one another in the world. In this paper, I suggest that today's English language arts classrooms can be sites of new discourses that question the 'taken-for-granted' views of the past and create spaces for new bodies of knowledge and social relationships alongside the old, traditional, and familiar.

Traditionally, English language arts classes in Canadian high schools have focused students' attention on the power of literature and language to stimulate imagination and to offer new understandings of 'self' and 'other.' Birkerts (1994), the North American writer and theorist, articulates one view of the power of literature: "Literary works," he writes, "have always derived their artistic value, their importance, from the fact that they comprehended the changing terms of our world and gave us narratives that could help us understand the forces impinging on our lives" (204). Literature, he believes, can offer students insights into events and experiences beyond their own world view and enable them to reflect on their own lives in reimagined ways. Manguel (1993), the Canadian writer and critic, reminds us that literature, in addition to its personal potential, also has political and social power:

> Words, literature, books, because of their very nature relentlessly challenge the right of those in power, ask unsettling questions, put in doubt our assumptions. Literature may not be able to save anyone from injustice, but something about it must be effective if every dictator, every totalitarian government, every threatened official tries to do away with it, by burning books, by banning books, by censoring books, by taxing books (xi).

What writers choose to represent through literature is always a political act. Narrative is never a neutral form, representing real or imaginary events, but a form that entails specific choices with distinct ideological and political implications. As Heble (1997) suggests, "Self-representational acts are narrative acts that construct a story of subjectivity and belonging and, in doing so, they have the power to shape the production, maintenance, and transmission of knowledge 'about' both self and other" (87).

> In the English language arts classroom, students are introduced to literature and language in the context of the discipline we call 'English' that has always been about more than acquiring basic skills. As an inherently political enterprise, 'English' is concerned with issues of representation of the world outside the classroom, dealing with ideas about society through the study of language and of selected texts.

Historically, "English" as a discipline is steeped in concerns about national identity and culture and about shifting notions of national communities. The discipline evolved in the nineteenth century from the British East India Company's desire to teach the native population in colonized India how to follow an "English way of life" and become good Company servants. As Eaglestone (2000) explains:

> The literature of England was seen as a *mould* of the English way of life, morals, taste and the English way of doing things: why not teach Indians how to be more English by teaching them English literature? Studying English literature was seen as a way of 'civilising' the native population (11).

Viswanathan (1987) suggests that British colonial administrators selected particular English texts to incorporate into the Indian curriculum on the basis that these texts were supported by 'noble Christian sentiments' and a sound morality. So, for example, Shakespeare was selected for the 'sound Protestant Bible principles' underpinning his texts, and writers such as Locke and Bacon were chosen for their 'scriptural morality.' These writings, Viswanathan explains, served to locate authority in the texts themselves and attempted to efface "the sordid history of colonialist expropriation, material expropriation, and class and race oppression behind European world dominance" (436). English literature was put forward as a way for Indians to "daily converse with the best and wisest Englishmen through the medium of their works" (437). These texts, Viswanathan contends, provided an ideal way for the British colonizers to bring together the desire for religious instruction promoted by missionaries in India, and the desire of the colonizers to communicate the laws of social order to the Indian people:

> British colonial administrators, provoked by missionaries on the one hand and fears of native insubordination on the other, discovered an ally in English literature to support them in maintaining control of the natives under the guise of a liberal education. With both secularism and religion appearing as political liabilities, literature appeared to represent a perfect synthesis of these two opposing positions. (434)

This idea of the study of English literature as a 'civilising force' was carried over into nineteenth-century Britain at the time of the Industrial Revolution. Educational advocates such as Matthew Arnold recommended that literary culture should be part of the school curriculum in order to educate the British 'common man' in 'civilised English.' Although the earliest degrees in 'English' in Britain focused more on the study of language, by 1917, Cambridge academics changed the degree to allow the study of English literature. These academics supported the study of literature as an invaluable way to promote the 'civilising' values of 'Englishness,' believing "that the study of literature would restore a sense of humanity to the world, in the face of the rampant growth of technology and the 'machine age'" (Eaglestone, 2000, p.14).

Arnoldian ideas about literature study as a humanizing activity were further mediated through the mid-twentieth century by T.S. Eliot, the American (and later naturalized English) critic, poet, and dramatist. Eliot supported the idea that certain literary texts have intrinsic artistic worth and should be read and studied without reference to history or time. As Widdowson (1999) explains,

> Eliot's notion of 'The Tradition,' while being highly selective . . . nevertheless harks back to Arnold's dictum of 'the best that has been thought and said in the world.' It is central in constructing the received mid-Twentieth-Century conception of 'Literature': a canon of great works which most successfully hold an essence of human experience in their poetic 'medium.' (p.49)

This notion of a canon of great works to be studied detached from their social and historical contexts became entrenched in universities and schools throughout Britain and the colonized world. Reinforced by the work of the critic F.R. Leavis, "English Literature" became the center of the education syllabus, enshrining the qualities of an essential 'Englishness' and attempting to hold "at bay the worst evils of contemporary life" (Widdowson, 1999, p. 56). A parallel movement in the United States, entitled 'New Criticism' similarly celebrated the uniqueness of the literary art object in and for itself while valuing the concept 'Literature' as "a select(ive) and valuable aesthetic and moral resource to replenish those living in the spiritual desert of mass civilisation" (Widdowson, 1999, p.59).

In North American classrooms today, the discipline of 'English' has expanded beyond a focus on literature and language to include multiple strands of the language arts. Yet, there remains in many classrooms a lingering nostalgia for the idea of 'authoritative texts' with assumptions of value and authenticity that clearly link the study of literature with the values of Western culture and life. These values, entrenched in a canon of literature still being taught in many contemporary classrooms, are "unquestioningly assumed to be universal human values, the most important values that apply to all people at all times and in all places" (Eaglestone, 2000, 54–55).

A curriculum of English language arts that relies on canonized Western texts and standard forms of English may appear universalist and apolitical on the surface, yet is in reality culturally specific. Historically bound and embedded within a

Eurocentric framework, this static kind of curriculum reflects a narrow view of a democratic society by authorizing narratives that consciously or unconsciously work towards a single voice, thereby repressing understanding of difference. Many such narratives work to develop unity through emphasizing symbolic differences between 'ourselves' and 'others' and exaggerating perceived distinctions of race and ethnicity.

The canonical cultural narratives of Western 'great books' exemplify this tendency by defining a particular and limited sense of collective national identity. The self-perpetuating nature of the canon means that the same texts tend to be taught again and again, year after year, and that these continue to play a significant role in creating a sense of national identity. The notion of the Western canon is further entrenched by contemporary literary critics such as Harold Bloom (1994) with his list of the thousand books that he believes all 'cultured' North Americans should have read. Bloom's list of texts, written predominantly by male, white writers from Britain, Europe, and the United States, reinforces a narrow view of citizenship and ignores the voices of writers and critics outside the white, middle-class mainstream. Despite the opposing views of African-American critics such as Toni Morrison (1992) and educators such as Arthur Applebee (1993), Bloom's list has helped to reinforce the teaching of canonized literature in North American schools.

Similarly, when Random House Modern Library asked its editorial board members in 1998 to compile a list of the one hundred best novels written in English in the twentieth century, they produced a highly publicized list of texts written almost exclusively by male, white writers from England and America. Only ten of the writers are women and there are very few writers of colour. Another "List of the Best of the Century" was solicited by Random House Modern Library from a readers' poll that opened on July 20, 1998 and closed on October 20, 1998. This list of novels, although more eclectic than the one developed by the editorial board, is dominated by texts that readers are likely to have encountered in school in Britain, Canada, or The United States over the past decades. Among the top twenty-five of this list are the following perennial favorite school novels: *To Kill a Mockingbird* by Harper Lee; *Animal Farm* and *1984* by George Orwell; *Brave New World* by Aldous Huxley; *The Catcher in the Rye* by J.D. Salinger; *The Grapes of Wrath* by John Steinbeck; and *Lord of the Flies* by William Golding. The compilation and widespread publicity accorded to such lists reinforces the view that these are the texts that are considered valuable for students to read in school and that they offer some enduring and universal insights into the nature of citizenship today. Eaglestone (200) explains one reason that this canon of school texts has such longevity and power:

> In English at all levels, the same canonical texts come up again and again, year after year. A person who studied English and has become a teacher often teaches the texts she or he was taught, in part because she or he was taught that these texts were the most important (p. 56).

In Canadian schools over the past twenty years, English language arts teachers have been encouraged to balance the teaching of such canonical British and American texts with Canadian literary texts that narrate their own story of nation. In many classrooms, the Canadian texts being taught are a handful of novels, short stories, and poems by white writers, most of which were published or anthologized during the 1970s and 1980s. Immigrant writers such as Mukherjee (1995) have critiqued the choice of these school literary texts. Mukherjee suggests that Canada's 'story of nation' was created through a national literature constructed "by powerful professors, bureaucrats, editors, publishers, and reviewers, the majority of them white males... under the aegis of nineteenth century European notions of nationhood" (par.8). According to these ideas, "a nation is considered as racially and culturally 'uniform', and a nation's literature has to reflect the 'soul' of the nation, its history and traditions" (par.8). Much of the literature that was published in the 1970s and is now being read in Canadian classrooms privileges what Mukherjee describes as "an all-white canon of works about small towns and wilderness, about white settlers pioneering on the frontier with the RCMP maintaining law and order" (par.9). Presented in universalist terms, this canon has been able to discount its whiteness and to hide its ability to shut out other voices and traditions.

A more fluid and hybrid curriculum of English language arts considers literary texts as having potential for critiquing ideas of the uniformity of nation. Such a curriculum has been made possible over the past three decades by destabilizing forces that have helped to problematize the notion of innate 'literary value' and to highlight the subjective and often arbitrary nature of literary evaluation. Foremost among these forces have been the feminist and postcolonial movements. Widdowson (1999) elaborates:

> [F]eminism and postcolonialism simultaneously deconstruct 'Literature' and the 'Western Canon' by exposing their partial and ideological nature; allow for a creative rereading of past 'classic' works; and bring into view other literatures (especially, but not exclusively, contemporary ones) which articulate hitherto occluded areas of experience from those who are constrained within conventional conspectus of 'Literature' (p.69).

A more open curriculum makes room for fictions of identity that provide a new perspective on the politics of identity and possibilities for resistance and transformation. In this curriculum there is always room for new stories, for narratives that allow for the power of the imagination to break through the taken-for-granted metanarrative of nation, Maxine Greene (1996) suggests that a curriculum that encourages diversity and openness is one in which students are invited into a democratic community where there is always space for new narratives and for personal engagement with the literature read in class. Greene elaborates:

> Engaging with works of fiction—children's literature, adult novels and stories—can contribute to the shaping of experience in the form of a story. There is great interest today in approaches to reading that encourage the participation of readers in the

production of meanings, rather than the unearthing of hidden meanings in texts. . . . We must, as Jean Paul Sartre has said, lend the book our lives. The meanings that we produce in so doing bring to light relations, patterns, and connections in our experience; we see more; we advance somehow in our quests. . . . [T]his kind of participation just described eventually may activate in readers the desire for *communitas* with others (37).

Students in such classes are welcomed into a "community-in the-making," a plurality of experiences where the "ragged edges of the real" (Greene, 1996, 40) demand representation and open up new spaces of possibilities for democracy and citizenship.

Greene's ideas resonate with those of Toni Morrison (1992) who reminds us that for decades the experiences of people outside the white mainstream have been the "invisible presence" in North American literature. This absence becomes visible when students are introduced to literature by previously marginalized writers and have opportunities to discuss different ways of understanding the world. Greene (1996) explains:

We and those we teach must have opportunities to make "different" experiences objects of our experience as we open texts—diverse stories, telling stories hitherto unknown and telling them well—and try to recognize what we have pushed aside. Opening spaces in our classrooms that enable all kinds of persons to appear before one another articulating the nature of their searches, we have to make available works that legitimize ways of being once disqualified, too long scorned: works by women, works by the newcomers streaming into this country, works by artists and writers displaying their own visions of what Dostoyevsky knew, and Flaubert, and Kant, and the Brontes (41).

Much of this literature opens up questions of citizenship and national identity. Canadian students who read texts such as Toni Morrison's *The Bluest Eye*, Wayson Choy's *The Jade Peony*, Anita Rau Badami's *Tamarind Mem*, or Pauline Johnson and Rudy Wiebe's *Stolen Life* can begin to question what it means to be a Canadian citizen in the twenty-first century. Such texts, as Dimitriadis and McCarthy suggest, offer us "new ways to think about community, ethics, and the responsibilities we all have to perform history, to make it relevant in the present tense" (79). They have the potential to "transform the old models, which ask teachers and students to come to terms with a fixed body of historical fact, into a view of history as partial, and part of a collective project in which we are all invested" (79). By reimagining history as a shared and unpredictable work in progress, students can begin to critically question previously taken-for-granted literary understandings and to challenge linear historical views of Western literature as the special provenance of white male writers.

Literary works, especially minority texts which are infused with references to historical and social realities, continue to perform as "acts of imaginative representation" (Tuzi, 1996, 88). Today's English language arts classrooms can move beyond the historical view of subject 'English' as a civilizing force that promotes unity and shuts out difference. Literature study offers the potential for a creative rereading of past 'classic' works and an exploration of contemporary texts in ways that expose their ideological nature and allow for dialogue on the multiple ways we understand ourselves as citizens and members of a democratic community.

References

Applebee, A. (1993). *Literature in the secondary school*. Research Report No. 25. Urbana, IL: National Council of Teachers of English.

Birkerts, Sven. (1994). *The Gutenberg elegies: The fate of reading in an electronic age*. New York: Faber and Faber.

Bloom, H. (1994). *The Western canon: The books and school of the ages*. New York: Riverhead Books.

Dimitriadis, G. & McCarthy, C. (2001). *Reading and teaching the postcolonial*. New York: Teachers College Press.

Eaglestone, R. (2000). *Doing English*. London and New York: Routledge.

Greene, M. (1996). Plurality, diversity, and the public space. In A. Oldenquist (Ed.), *Can democracy be taught* (pp. 27–44). Bloomington, IN: Phi Delta Kappa Educational Foundation.

Manguel, A. (1993). Introduction. In C. Stephenson (Ed.), *Countries of invention: contemporary world writing* (pp. viii–xi). Toronto: Addison-Wesley Publishers Ltd.

Morrison, T. (1992). *Playing in the dark: whiteness and the literary imagination*. New York: Vintage Books.

Mukherjee, A. (1995). Canadian nationalism, Canadian literature, and racial minority women. *Essays on Canadian Writing, 56*, 78–96.

Tuzi, M. (1996). Theorizing minority texts: Cultural specificity, agency and representation. *Canadian Ethnic Studies, XXVII (3)*, 85–94.

Viswanathan, G. (1987). The beginnings of English literary study in British India. *Oxford Literary Review* 9, 1–2.

Widdowson, P. (1999). *Literature*. London and New York: Routledge.

III

TROUBLING BODIES IN CITIZENSHIP EDUCATION

Kent den Heyer

DEFINING PRESENCE AS AGENTS OF SOCIAL LIFE AND CHANGE

> *And as imagination bodies forth the forms of*
> *things unknown,*
> *the poet's pen turns them to shapes*
> *And gives airy nothing*
> *A local habitation and name*
> —SHAKESPEARE, *A midsummer night's dream. Act V, Scene 1*

The great bard could not have described better what is at stake in the teaching of history. History is the school subject most entrusted with the creation of nation from airy nothing to an "imagined community" and the transformation of individual students into knowledgeable and committed (patriotic) citizens. To the degree national communities are imagined, we must attend to the poetics of power and pen to name and to give "airy nothing a local habitation and name."

School history brings forth the forms of things unknown as "names of history" (Ranciere, 1994). In the form of names, school history idealizes national identity and citizenship into racial and gendered (amongst other descriptors) norms (Stanley, 1998). Scott writes that "identities don't pre-exist their strategic political invocations" (Scott, 2001, p. 285). As I have noted elsewhere (den Heyer, 2003a), Scott's work explores the ways in which the political category of "women," as a group with rights to participate in political places, "was not so much a self-evident fact of history as it was evidence—from particular and discrete moments in time—of someone's, some group's efforts to identify and thereby mobilize a collectivity" (Scott, 2001, p. 287). Historians, she argues, invoke present identifications through the historical task of retrospectively asserting categories of identity—of names—with which to engage the archive: in her work of "unruly" women who disrupt(ed) the policing of language, status, and identity. There are few examples more noteworthy of that policing than provincially or state-approved textbooks and teachers who rely on such sources for the content of historical imaginings. It is these same textbooks that give the nation a habitation in time and a domesticated space populated with idealized agents. It is to the question of idealized agents in the theorizing of citizenship to which I now wish to turn.

The idealizations of citizenship and civic education are found in debates between liberal and civic republican theorists. Both liberal and civic republican theorists of citizenship attempt to answer what it means to be a citizen by defining lists of virtues good citizens should possess (Callan, 1997). They differ, however, as to whether such possessions should serve to protect and enhance a private or public domain. Liberals argue that the pursuit of the good life is a private affair. Civic republicans argue the good life ought to be sought in the community. While debate exists, especially in the Canadian context, about the legitimacy of a special status for religious and ethnic groups, in each case citizenship is first and foremost considered a relationship between a citizen endowed with rights and responsibilities and a state supposedly neutral as to questions of the good life.

While important, such debates prescribe virtues rather than describe the living complexities of students' lives and the role of historical imagining in casting their present intelligible and futures possible. In doing so, those engaged in such debates idealize a future citizenship as well as traditional history teaching does the past, and, as I will illustrate further below, the nation and great men as agents of national life.

Such idealizations of citizenship ignore the ways that school history might inform students' capacities as agents of social life and change. Several objectives I argue are served by engaging this ignorance. The first is the need to ground studies of the past in terms of students' present imagined and material relationships. The relational dynamics of individuality and of representation and reality—in social psychology, postmodernity, and postcolonial discourses for example—have been well described; although the degree to which theoretical insights have impacted the study of the past in schools is questionable (den Heyer, 2004). If historical study does not serve to enhance students' intelligibility as agents of social life, then it serves to conscript them into its present order of idealized names.

A second objective is to attend to the influence on social life and change not only of grand gestures, but of the seemingly small habits, utterances, and stances in relationships that create the context of social norms as well as the possibility of their disruption. The need for a more complex approach to questions of civic relationships, or as I argue, our relationships as agents of social life, is evident from recent research investigating the ways students interpret the human influences in social change.

A recently published review of history and social studies research is prescient. It investigated what the research into historical understandings indicates about the ways that students of various ages interpret agency and social change. I summarize the findings as follows:

- As in any one of thousands of movies about macho heroic agents, most students cast celebrated individuals as the cause of social change.
- Agency is the expression of individual desires or motivations played out in a social domain characterized by individual power struggles.
- Social change occurred because celebrated agents rescued the masses from their stupidity or simple backwardness.
- Students personalize political structures as the extension of powerful individuals' desires and goals (den Heyer, 2003b).

In these explanations the agency of heroic individuals appears to be teleological in nature, social change devoid of life's contingency, and exclusionary social arrangements the product of individual misunderstandings.

Given the immensity of challenges so many collectively face (e.g., struggles for peace, economic and environmental sustainability, more inclusive definitions of, and material benefit for, communities) and most people's more modest zones of influence, this hyperindividualized heroic and idealized notion of agency likely contributes to the widely acknowledged political apathy of youth. Further to this point, and as I have explored elsewhere (den Heyer, 2003c), an idealized past promotes an illiteracy of individuality–our indebtedness to the social movements struggling over the terms by which we explain ourselves. Such illiteracy is evident when those privileged by race, class, gender, or sexual orientation simply cannot or refuse to appreciate that "success" and survival may result from forces more complex than individual hard work.

Social psychologists would be unsurprised by findings about the ways that students reason about agency and social change. Drawing from their synoptic review of research in social psychology and their own empirical studies, the social psychologists Markus and Kitayama describe the most widely propagated model of agency in a North American and Western European public sphere utilized by students in their explanations of social change:

- Normatively 'good' actions should emanate from an individual's own desires, goals, intentions, or choices;
- Agency is bounded within an independent self, foregrounded as the source of motivations and action; groups and networks are fixed in the background.

- This model of agency as disjoint, or as disconnected from others and rooted solely in the individual, is widely distributed and inscribed in mainstream American society. It is expressed by social scientists, reflected in the media, and echoed by individuals talking about themselves. (Markus and Kitayama, 2002, p. 6)*

This model is insufficient as a basis for working with students to describe the human actions involved in social life and change. From a pedagogical perspective, it fails to sufficiently honour the complexities of human subjectivity and the group struggles to name and provide subjectivity with content. From a disciplinary perspective, the same insufficiency is evident as "presentism" when students apply this contemporary model backwards in time to explain social change.

From a cultural and social psychological perspective (Wertsch, 1998), the common nationalist Whig narratives around which the past is so often wrapped–premised on teleological progress led by the great men of formal political power–helps explain why students interpret social change and agency in such stark terms. That textbooks (Willinsky, 1998) and teachers rely so extensively on such premises indicates the historical struggle and success of certain interests to represent the past and efficacious citizenship in their own name.

A veteran teacher in the U.S studied by S.G. Grant, a scholar of history education and research into historical understanding, usefully illustrates the presentation of this Whig narrative with its concomitant "American middle class" ideal of agency. George Blair (a pseudonym) is a European-American teacher at a suburban school, where 80% of students move on to postsecondary study, grew up in a working-class background, and holds a Master's degree in U.S. history and in social studies education.

Blair believes that students will not understand U.S. history unless he offers a trajectory of U.S. history "from colonials to Clinton." He conveys U.S. history as a meaningful whole, rather than explore meaningful narrative holes occupied by traditionally excluded historical groups and struggles. As Grant writes, Blair offers a narrative filled with "standard historical fare:"

> [H]ighlight[ing] stories of individuals' actions and experiences. Dates, places, and events are prominent, but they serve primarily as the backdrop for stories of individual uncertainty, folly, courage, and determinations. (Grant, 2003, p. 12)

---

*It is crucial to note that Markus and Kitayama, and indeed the field of social psychology, do not make an argument that only one model can be found in a given society. Alternative representations exist in all societies. Their point rather is that one model tends to be privileged through greater distribution in multiple sites of social representation. Such dominant models of agency, and concomitant statements about relationships between individuals and collectives, indeed distinguish one from another society.

In a textbook example of what Wertsch & Rozen (1998) call "official" history, Blair populates his narrative monologue with the standard fare of political names, government policies, and events that occupy the formal sites of political power. Those influential social movements and groups outside these sites are relatively insignificant in Blair's view of U.S. history.

Blair offers a narrative that elides the complexity of agency and social life and change. As a central agent in his narrative, Blair personifies the U.S. nation-state, often speaking in terms of "we" that ignores the discontinuities, conflicts, and struggles over such a totalizing pronoun for which history and social studies instruction is rightly maligned: "Eisenhower also confronts the Soviets.... We hate the Soviet Union, we fear the Soviet Union.... We've got the H-bomb but we're scared as hell" (classroom lecture, Grant, 2003, p. 8). In an interview with Grant, Blair discusses his view of U.S. history. Again, note the reflexive use of "we," a pronoun that should be as much a question of historical study as it is its starting point:

> I think World War One is probably a watershed where we try to stay isolated. But in a very short time, we realize that you can't do it. You are out there and you're a leader and you must, if you have certain value judgments, you must bring those to the world, and try to make a better place out of it (Grant, 2003, p. 159).

The groups in the past and today contesting in whose name the U.S. government speaks through its domestic and foreign policies are not part of Blair's Whig narrative. As Grant notes, Blair tells a good story, and like many a good tale, Blair does not let the complexity of who "we" might be get in the way.

Blair emphasizes the importance of the civil rights era, not as the name given to a struggle against enforced social inequality benefiting and contested by a range of social groups, but as rather another cold war challenge faced by the Eisenhower administration caused by the *Brown* decision. From a lecture to students, it appears that this struggle was merely a legal one:

> The Brown decision overturns Plessy ... Brown says that schools, when they segregate, do harm to the black population and segregation must end.... (voice rising) and it starts the major movement toward civil rights in the South that continues to today ... (Grant, 2003, p. 11).

The crucial historical fact missing here is that that legal challenge was launched by an *already existing* and widely distributed social movement against institutionalized white racism: the policing of who may appear and under what circumstances in social spaces.

Rather, students are presented with a prescriptive vision of history that appears to be one and the same as the past and with little about its veracity to question. It is a textbook representation in which heroic agents are "foregrounded as the source of action while others are fixed in the background." It is also a narrative with not only implications for the ways that students envision agency, but one that has nothing to offer them in terms of insights into their own capacities of social life

90 | Troubling Bodies in Citizenship Education

and change and under whose name they will cast their social commitments. It is of little use, however, to blame teachers who more often than not and to no small degree present students what they themselves have been taught. What I argue is needed are accessible formulations that describe the ways in which presentations of the past invoke present identifications and emotional commitments. It is to one such formulation that I now turn.

Historical Agency

To explore our variegated capacities as agents of social life and change requires a formulation of agency that attends to the relationship between the historical names in which the past is cast and individual interpretation of identity and social life. As explored in earlier work (den Heyer, 2004) and building on the work of the sociologists Emirbayer and Mische (1998), I define "individual agency" as *an imaginative capacity for shaping intentions, forming choices, and undertaking actions*. This capacity consists of three moments, or "chords" consisting of "iteration," "practical-evaluation," and "projectivity" (Emirbayer and Mische, 1998). What is noteworthy in my definition and the moments depicted by Emirbayer and Mische is the way that this model of agency puts in relation the storied past and expected future, two crucial dimensions of student inquiry for history and citizenship education.

To briefly review, "iteration" is the selective reactivation and incorporation of past patterns of thought and action into practical activity. It is reiteration that gives order, they argue, to "social universes" and "sustain[s] identities, interactions, and institutions over time" (Emirbayer and Mische, 1998, p. 971). In this moment, students draw upon materialized memory (e.g., movies, textbooks, family stories, statues, holidays) as cultural resources guiding sense-making activities. The "practical-evaluative" capacity refers to the "practical and normative judgments among alternative possible trajectories of action, in response to the emerging demands, dilemmas, and ambiguities of presently evolving situations" (Emirbayer and Mische, 1998, p. 971). In this moment, cultural resources help define present situations and future-oriented goals, or "projectivity." "Projectivity" refers to "the imaginative generation by actors of possible future trajectories of action, in which received structures of thought and action (or materialized memory) may be creatively reconfigured in relation to actors' hopes, fears, and desires for the future" (Emirbayer and Mische, 1998, p. 971).

Projectivity involves a movement of what Mead (1932) named as the "desirous imagination" which, as Scott (2001) notes about feminist historical work, moves to encompass a past in the name of the future. This "desirous imagination" is a response "to the challenges and uncertainties of social life [whereby agents] distance themselves from the schemes, habits, and traditions that constrain social identities and institutions" (Emirbayer and Mische, 1998, p. 984). As they note, "[t]he key to grasping the dynamic possibilities of human agency is to view it as composed of variable and changing orientations within the flow of time" (Emirbayer and Mische,

1998, p. 964). "Changing orientations" are the divided attention to moments—interation, evaluation, and projectivity–in imaginative acts of sense making.

It is clear with this formulation that, in contrast to a predominant American middle-class ideal, agency is not simply "bounded within" individuals. Rather, it is a capacity whose expression relies on collective conceptual resources. Schutz (1967) calls these images, ideals, and terms that individuals iterate in their sense-making activities a society's "stocks of knowledge." Culturally specific models of agency identified in the studies of social psychologists exemplify such sense-aiding stocks (Markus and Kitayama, 2002; Morris et al., 2001).

To investigate social change adequately requires a broader and more collective interpretation of agency than that provided by the American middle-class model; one that historicizes the content of, and struggles to materialize the memory that individuals iterate to evaluate or make sense of their actions. I define "historical agency" as *a capacity expressed by groups in struggles over the conceptual resources that individuals use to interpret social and material life (e.g., interpretations of personal and social goals, terms individuals use to define and express their identities, representations of iconic role models, disciplinary interpretations)* (den Heyer, 2004). A cartoon helps to illustrate the changing conceptual resources available to individuals that result from historical agency:

> The cartoon shows three people sitting at three desks in an office. All the words in the cartoon are in thought bubbles. The first person on the left is thinking, "The vibrations are over-whelming. Two white people are afraid of a smart, aggressive African-American!" The second person, sitting at her desk in the center of the cartoon, is thinking, "I'm sick of their patronizing, macho glances. They can't stand a woman in a responsible position!" The third person sitting at his desk to the right is thinking, "I can see it in their eyes. They don't like me because I'm gay!"

Each person depicted in the cartoon identifies as a member of a group that has waged struggles over who may legitimately appear in the preferred spaces of social life and garner their concomitant material rewards. Each reiterates these terms to evaluate or interpret their present situation so as to guide a projected course of future-oriented action (options each may take, for example, to resolve the discomfort). "African-American," "woman," or "gay" are terms that did not articulate social and political positions for their grandmothers and grandfathers. What changed between then and now? In what ways did such definitions of presence and interpretations of social situations as illustrated in the cartoon become available?"

These sense-aiding "stocks of knowledge" became available through the historical agency expressed by groups in costly struggles over "the names of history." In addition to strikes, legal challenges, protests, and civil disobedience, to give their claims for participation in local or national life coherence required that these groups locate themselves temporally in the present between a historical past and projected future: a documented past of oppression and an imagined future in which the struggle, in these cases, against white, male, or heterosexual social and material privilege, ceases to exist (Scott, 2001; Young, 1990). I chose to name this agency "historical," even though it is a broadly distributed capacity, because of what is at stake in these struggles. Whose names and images, ideals, and terms will constitute significant "historical" subjects with the legitimacy and cachet assigned such status?

These struggles continue today as does the work of competing groups to write their names and ideals of citizenship into the history taught in schools. Little effort is required to identify whose images, ideals, and terms dominate that history, at least in textbooks, movies, and in the corporate press. The challenge of teaching about social change and the ways that citizens impact social life, however, is not just to represent greater diversity as teachers tell narratives of progressive national inclusion in which a particular vision of the individual, state, and society in the present are simply given:

> [W]hen rights have been granted, the first operation of the political order [is] to initiate a process of forgetfulness by virtue of which persons come to possess rights not because they were victimized or because they fought for them, but because they are *individuals,* i.e., abstracted persons. (Alejandro, 1993, p. 15)

This challenge is to connect past and present social struggles and the particular historical names by which we make ourselves, others, and the present intelligible (e.g. gay, straight, bi, black, white, African-American, feminist, Canadian, American). Doing so highlights exactly what is at stake for interpretations of citizenship in the teaching and learning of history.

Agency Rather Than Citizenship

I have argued that, without attending to students' sense of agency, the debate in citizenship remains far removed from the complexities of students' lives and the complexity of social life. As I believe the cartoon helps illustrate, both civic and liberal ideals of citizenship insufficiently describe the ways that people participate in social life and change through their sense-making activities, that is, how social change emerges from personal identifications with groups whose struggles contribute to changes in who counts as citizens (e.g., peasant, aristocracy, racialized groups, women), or whose practices or ways of life will be recognized as worthy of protection (i.e., gay marriage, religiously significant dress). In these struggles, citizenship is itself a contested ideal rather than a posited fact, what is fought over as much as a guaranteed position from which one fights.

In contrast to citizenship, a concept of historical agency assists investigation of the multiple zones-of-influence in which people contribute to the social life of their communities, sometimes supporting and sometimes contesting norms, sometimes doing so simultaneously and unknowingly, sometimes in the domain of their professional work but not in regards to their family life, and sometimes vice versa. The purpose of engaging questions of agency and social change rather than citizenship is twofold. As previously mentioned, such questions offer students the opportunity to connect historical study and their variegated capacities in the multiple social relationships in which they live (i.e., family, as sexual beings, workers). The historical constitutes one source that provides ideals and terms to interpret social relationships. It is therefore vital that students are provided opportunities to connect the history they encounter in schools to the broader social struggles over in whose name the past is cast.

Why Social Change?

The emphasis on social change is crucial. I write of "social" in contrast to "historical" or "political" change for two reasons. In his widely cited discussion of nationalism and nations as imagined communities, Anderson specifically employs "social" rather than any other descriptor of change:

> In the preceding chapters I have tried to delineate the processes by which the nation came to be imagined, and, once imagined, adapted and transformed. Such an analysis has necessarily been concerned primarily with social change and different forms of consciousness. But it is doubtful whether either social change or transformed consciousness, in themselves, do much to explain the *attachment* that people feel for the inventions of their imaginations—or, to revive a question raised at the beginning of this text–why people are ready to die for these inventions. (Anderson, 2001, p. 229, italics in original)

Anderson's impressive analysis covers a wide range of technological, economic, political, and intellectual changes many refer to as "historical." Why then did he choose "social" change?

While I can only speculate as to his reasons for this choice, it appropriately reflects his focus on the imaginary life of communities and the material effects of members willing to kill or die in their name. As my concern is with agency as an imaginative capacity shaped through communities, a focus on social change is likewise appropriate. Like Anderson's "imagined communities," agency is an imaginative and social capacity. Rather than the vagueness of Anderson's "forms of consciousness," however, I write of this capacity as one expressed through a stock of images, ideals, and terms that agents reiterate in evaluating their social world in the present and their projecting of future imaginings.

Another reason for using "social" change is my hope to implicate students in the present as agents of their communities. For example, it is one thing to study the emergence of racism in conjunction with the trading and colonizing efforts of the European sea powers in the 16th to 19th centuries or the resistance of many whites to black civil rights, or, as an apprehension expressed in its patriarchal form, the resistance of those privileged by gender against full material recognition of women's rights. It is quite another for students to inquire into how such a racialized and misogynist world contributes to their present emotional life and to the ways they define themselves and their communities. "Social" connotes my belief that historical study ought to connect past practices of inequality to the present order of names: to the poetics of power and pen that give "airy nothing a local habitation and name."

References

Anderson, B. (2001). Imagined communities: Reflections on the origin and spread of nationalism, in S. Seidman & J. C. Alexander (Eds.), *The new social theory reader*, pp. 224–230. London: Routledge.

den Heyer, K. (2003a). Historical agency and social change: Something more than 'symbolic' empowerment, in L. Allen, D. Breault, D. Cartner, B. Setser, M. Hayes, R. Gaztambide-Fernandez & K. Krasny (Eds.), *Curriculum and pedagogy for peace and sustainability*, pp. 111–112. Troy, New York: Educators International Press.

den Heyer, K. (2003b). Between every 'now' and 'then': A role for the study of historical agency in history and citizenship education. *Theory and Research in Social Education*, 31(4), 411–434.

den Heyer, K. (2003c). The historical agency of Ted. T. Aoki in scholarly fugues, communities and change. *Educational Insights*, 8(2), [Available:http://www.ccfi.educ.ubc.ca/publication/insights/v08n02/aoki/denheyer.html].

den Heyer, K. (2004). *A critical case sampling of the ways teachers interpret the human agency behind social change*. Manuscript under review.

Callan, E. (1997). *Creating citizens: Political education and liberal democracy*. Oxford: Clarendon Press.

Grant, S.G. (2003). *History lessons: Teaching, learning, and testing in U.S. high school classrooms*. Mahwah, NJ: Lawrence Erlbaum Associates.

Markus, H. R. & Kitayama, S. (2002). Models of Agency: Sociocultural diversity in the construction of action. Draft prepared for V. Murphy-Berman and J. Berman (Eds.), *The 49th annual Nebraska symposium on motivation: Cross cultural differences in perspectives on self*.

Mead, G.H. (1932). *The philosophy of the present*. Chicago: University of Chicago Press.

Morris, M. W., Menon, T. & Ames, D. R. (2001). Culturally conferred conceptions of agency: A key to social perception of persons, groups, and other actors. *Personality and Social Psychology Review*, 5(2), 169–182.

Rancière, J. (1994). *The names of history* (H. Melehy, Trans.). Minneapolis: University of Minnesota Press.

Schutz, A. (1967). *The phenomenology of the social world* (G. Walsh & F. Lehnert, Trans.). Evanston, IL: Northwestern University Press.

Scott, J. W. (2001). Fantasy echo: History and the construction of identity. *Critical Inquiry*, 27, 285–304.

Stanley, T. (1998). The struggle for history: historical narratives and anti-racist pedagogy. *Discourse: studies in the cultural politics of education*, 19(1), 41–51.

Wertsch, J. V. (1998). *Mind as action*. New York: Oxford University Press.

Wertsch, J. V., & Rozin, M. (1998). Russian Revolution: Official and unofficial accounts, in J. Voss & M. Carretero (Eds.), *Learning and reasoning in history: International review of history education*, pp. 83–97. London: Woburn Press.

Willinsky, J. (1998). *Learning to divide the world: Education at empire's end*. Minneapolis: University of Minnesota Press

Young, R.(1990). *White mythologies: Writing history and the West*. London: Routledge.

Lori B. Macintosh and Lisa W. Loutzenheiser

QUEERING CITIZENSHIP

What's in a Name?

There are complex power relations concerning notions of the citizen and citizenship in curricula and classrooms. For better or worse, citizenship is tied to individual subjectivity and is dictated, in large part, by one's public belonging and sociopolitical placement. For some, citizenship is a seemingly innocuous term that means very little in their day-to-day lives; while for others, it is a term rife with political tension and hidden oppressions. In both social and political terms, one of the most powerful designations one can claim, or be given, is that of *citizen*.

Citizenship, in the context of education and curricula, can be understood as political identity in association with nation, belongingness, and the inherent rights and freedoms that accompany such a membership. Yet, it can also be understood as community, the rights and freedoms that one assumes and observes as a member of a given community. This is a concept of citizenship, and of citizen, that questions binaries of inclusion/exclusion and pushes at the boundaries of hegemonic ideologies. That is, defined as such, citizenship proposes to acknowledge both a larger public and the diverse subjectivities of its members, moving beyond incitements to normativism and conformity. This is a discourse of citizenship that we propose can be rendered visible through the lens of queer theory and is useful for engaging citizenship as it pertains to marginalized populations and issues of queer students, in particular.

In this chapter, we propose to read citizenship through sexuality and schooling as one avenue to explore how educators can begin to facilitate a dialogue where sexually marginalized youth feel recognized and included. We argue that queer theories, and the queering of theory, offers educators and educational theorists sites of contestation that might open up pedagogical and curricular projects which unsettle heteronormativity in schooling. At the outset, we discuss how our reading of queer theory and identify its usefulness for thinking about schools and student bodies. It is imperative to the well-being of all students that educators begin to acknowledge the school as being part of a larger social system and the systemic nature of the heterocentric ideology in which it is embedded. Next, these notions are explored through a reading of citizenship, heteronormativity, and queer bodies in educational settings. Thereafter, the silences within queer theory are discussed. Lastly, we suggest a reconceptualization of the queer citizen and its usefulness to educators and youth.

Queered Theory, Student Bodies, and School Spaces

"Queer" as a term, as opposed to gay, lesbian, or bisexual purposefully disrupts the notion that identity is fixed or immutable (Butler, 1993b). Theoretically, it serves to highlight and disrupt the ubiquity of the heteronormative (Sumara & Davis, 1999; Warner, 1993). Within this chapter, queer is used discretely from gay and lesbian, and GLBTQI (gay, lesbian, bisexual, transgender, questioning, and intersex) as distinct from either. Each categorization has its own set of historical contexts and purposes, the complexities of which cannot be adequately addressed here (see Thomas, 2000). Our purpose is not to further infuse queer with set meanings; rather, our use of the term queer relies on fluid, deliberately partial, and intersecting notions of identity (Berlant & Warner, 1998; Butler, 1993a).

Queer theory takes as its premise an unsettling of identities. It aids in complicating an often overly simplified notion of the gay "role model" and the loose insertion of gay and lesbian issues in curricular materials. There are dangers stemming from the current lack of curriculum, but equally perilous is the reckless inclusion of gay and lesbian content without the necessary contextualization. When used uncritically, such insertions encourage a reification of gay/straight binaries rather than fostering a desire to move beyond the ideological trappings of heteronormativity and universalized identities.

As a critical tool, queer theory offers a panoramic lens through which to view the complications of identity formation. Youth do not benefit from the proliferation of one-dimensional categorizations or essentialized identity constructions. It is our assertion that queer theory offers educators and students a tool to look at schools, classrooms, educational settings, and their individual inhabitants contextually, beyond universalizations and discrete particulars. It does so through a rejection of asexualizing, assimilationist strategies which argue that the only way to gain rights or citizenship is to cling to and maintain a logic that queer people are the same as, or ought to desire to be the same as, non-queers. Notably, queer theory requires an ongoing interrogation of heteronormativity and an acknowledgment of the constantly changing nature of our relationships to terms such as queer, gay, lesbian, transgender, etcetera (Talburt, 2000). Within this, there is an assumption of complex power relations concerning notions of citizenship in curricula and classrooms.

For better or worse, citizenship is tied to individual subjectivity and is dictated, in large part, by one's public belonging and sociopolitical placement. In terms of the classroom, this sociopolitical placement has significance both inside and outside the school. Queer theory, in this context, does not emanate from pluralistic notions that imagines sameness or the erasure of difference as the goal, nor is it an add-in model for re/creating new and substitutive categories of identity. It is a political and theoretical structuring and an intellectual fault line that acknowledges difference and along which the potential for slippage and rupture is ever-present. Within this theoretical framework, what one is called or named and how one chooses to identify oneself, even transiently, is acknowledged as a vital component of agency and citizenship.

Educational settings are not monolithic spaces functioning within a neutral social setting. They are made up of scores of different communities, identity groupings interacting in a complex morass of competing wants and needs, often in tension. Yet both materially and discursively, these spaces have normalizing tendencies and regulatory functions. Both the erasure of queer youth and the boundaried acknowledgment of queer youth as citizens act as normalizing apparatus. Here, normalizing has, at its base, a desire to regulate and erase differences from within society's dominant framework. Simultaneously, the dominant (in this case heterosexuality) needs the Other; it is this Other through which the heteronormative maintains its status. The calling out of gay and lesbian bodies (but rarely queer), even through their erasure, transforms an often indeterminate and invisible queer body into a newly "identified" and pathologized form. It is the ever-present threat of 'calling out,' defined by universalized generalizations that, in turn, limit one's ability and one's political mobility within the classroom, lunchroom, and playing field.

Sexual minority and other marginalized students make the case that all youth benefit from spaces in schools where they can be acknowledged and self-identify without fear of harassment, shame, or intimidation (Loutzenheiser, 2001, 2002). These spaces are of particular import for students, such as sexual minority youth, whose very identities are either erased or misnamed in schools (MacIntosh, 2004). The importance of 'being seen' as representative of, belonging to, having the ability to attain rights, or a "place at the table" cannot be underestimated. While many schools have instituted some form of multicultural education program or emphases, the majority do not address the concerns of queer youth within the official curriculum (Crocco, 2001; Kumashiro, 2001; Lee et al., 1994; Pagenhart, 1994). These missing discourses suggest to queer youth that they are not worthy of inclusion, that they are and ought to remain invisible. This is not a call for "inclusive" curricula that merely adds an appetizer to the curricular menu, a toothsome addition that has little or no connection to the main meal. It is an acknowledgment that "being seen" is necessary and that spaces where the attainment of rights and the acceptance of difference are recognized and the gaps of missing discourses are exposed offer students a respite from hostile school environments. A desire for curricular and pedagogical inclusivity in-and-of-itself is not a useful framework for queering a discourse of citizenship. As is the case with antiracist and multicultural discourses, inclusivity borne of heteronormative social institutions too often means that the resulting assimilationist decoupage simply covers over the ideological mechanisms of oppression. Uncritical inclusivity reifies the Other and reinforces the status quo, leaving those "outside," with few access points into curricular conversations that acknowledge power relations and imbalances. As a vital component of a reconceptualized curriculum, the language of social justice is suited to speak to an ascendant metapublic desire for assimilation and immobilization.

Within schools, youth embody certain cultural norms, normative values, and binary mechanisms of exclusion/inclusion, all of which are microcosms within a larger socio-political system. As private identities emerge and individual bodies come to be understood and articulated, they collide with and within the boundaried public arena of the classroom. Relying on readings of schools that complicate, disrupt, and note the erasures inherent within the construction of private (e.g. nonnormative sexualities) and public (e.g. heteronormative identity), we argue that queer theories and the queering of theory offer educators sites of contestation through which to open up pedagogical and curricular potential and unsettle heteronormativity in schooling.

Heteronormativity in the Classroom

Within the classroom, heterosexuality is a given, as are the binary categorizations of sex and gender. The classroom is also host to numerous other boundaried and dichotomized assumptions, the most obvious of which is public and private. All are limited by the formulaic restrictions of heteronormative discourse. Giroux (2003) notes that education is a democratic public sphere. That is, children enter into the classroom as public citizens, their private lives seemingly inconsequential to their participation, unless as individuals, they fail to fit tidily within dominant identity frameworks. Recent studies note that more gay and lesbian youth are self-identifying as such in high school, even though schools remain spaces where verbal, physical, and social harassment is often the result (Gay Lesbian and Straight Education Network, 2003). These queer students do not fit neatly; their private is made public and is the defining mechanism of their *publicness*. Berlant and Warner (1998) argue that the private or personal becomes both a self-defining mechanism and a means by which the queer, gay, or lesbian body is named and politically circumscribed. Here, we are suggesting that both the private and the public are privileged, ordered, *and* proscribed differently depending on whether one's identity is being claimed or assigned. While both the public and personal remain always in play, the structuring of one's social and political life is contingent upon heterosexual modes of address.

Where then does a queer body, a body not easily assimilated, locate itself in a public, heterosexual, historically masculine curricular space? As Warner (2002) suggests, regardless of its own subjectivity and social positioning, the queer body is bounded by its relegation to the private sphere. The queer body is private, hidden, and hypersexualized in both the private and public realm. Whether or not a self-identified queer student chooses to be "out," her identity is named, albeit silently, by the myriad social norms to which she does not adhere. Paradoxically, the student is also named through the Othering that is ubiquitous to a marginalized public identification. When viewed from the intersectionalities of race, class, ability, or religion, it becomes increasingly evident that the entry doors to civic life often slam shut upon the queer body's approach, especially when the queer body in question deviates further and further from the mythical norms of citizenry.

Complicating Discourses: Silences within Queer Theory

While there is much about the frameworks offered by queer theory that are useful to discussions of citizenship, sexual minority youth, and schools, it is not a field without criticism (Giffney, 2004; Kumashiro, 2001; Turner, 2000). Johnson (2001) argues that by neglecting the interrelationships between race, sexuality, and class that queer theory has "failed to live up to its full critical potential" (p. 18). He also notes that this lack is both theoretical and epistemological as queer theory either ignores race or relies too heavily on discursive analyses that neglect to explore the material with equal thoroughness. While one might argue with Johnson about the ability to separate the material from the discursive, his and others' concerns about the lack of interrogation regarding issues of race within queer theories must be acknowledged. While some, but certainly not all, queer theorists fail to discuss race explicitly, it is important to note that conversations about the silences of that which is not marked, are nonetheless conversations about race. Within this, however, it if fair to say that whiteness, or the normativity of whiteness, remains unexamined. The queer theories through which we are reading student sexuality and citizenship, acknowledge that gender, sexuality, race, class, and ethnicity are interconnected and do interact, which produces a wide array of mutable identities that resist rigid definition. In order to both address and disrupt the multiple meanings of heteronormativity within educational settings, issues of gender, sex, sexuality, heteronormativity, and race must be attended to with ideologically specific, intersecting, and rigorous critical methods.

For example, constructions of masculinity and femininity regulate how race is performed and perceived, and race, in turn, regulates gender (Mac An Ghaill, 1993). People of colour are an Other against which gender propriety is measured. Either they are "less than," which is not masculine or feminine enough or they are "simultaneously, cast as hyper masculine, as sexually aggressive . . . thus black men [are] depicted as rampaging sexual beasts, women carnivorously carnal, and gay men as sexually insatiable . . ." (Kimmel, 2000, p. 216). In similar ways, Asian American/Canadian men are often represented as being asexual, and Asian American/Canadian women are often seen as exotic, submissive, and willing to please. Asian males are viewed as asexual because they are perceived as not conforming to how a (white) man would or ought to perform. Differing from the portrait of the imaginary "typical male," he is to be placed outside of what is masculine, that is, asexual or feminine. The norm against which the performance of one's gender and sexuality is measured is that of dominant culture, which brings pressure to bear on racial assimilation or conformity. If a racialized body is ultimately a gendered or sexualized Other, its very existence polices the bounds of normativity. Again, this mythical but regulating norm is measured against the heteronormative, white, authentically male body. Within our classrooms, this speaks to pedagogies, school culture, and citizenship.

Entertaining a Queer Citizenry

There are a number ways in which what we have identified as queer citizenship is not imagined to be a part of multicultural education in Canada and the United States. Because it is often not *imagined* as having a place within multicultural or even antiracist discourses, the queer body, in its racialized, class-based, ethnically diverse subjectivities has limited points of access within these dialogues. Many K-12 settings have begun to infuse curricula with semisubstantive notions of social justice; however, gay and lesbian "issues" are treated as pedagogical isolates, focused on just long enough to substantiate a politics of Otherness—leaving the queer body in a paralytic state of quasisubjectivity. The absence of a right of entry can result in the lack of a discernable voice, a political presence, a "legitimate" civic identity, and as a result one's identity as citizen *proper* is greatly compromised.

While the arguments can never be parallel, nor the politics of race and sexuality necessarily aligned, there is much to be gained from a fluid analysis of queer and antioppressive theories. As Shane Phelan (2001) also argues, one powerful congruence between issues of race and sexuality and their multiple intersections is an understanding of what it is to be understood, and are read as, both Other and citizen within the greater public imaginary. Antiracist discourses, particularly those that employ antioppressive strategies, offer a vastly different understanding of what it is to be a citizen. Such discourses acknowledge that being recognized as citizen does not automatically or universally bestow upon the recipient the ability to participate equally in the public sphere, to engage in civil discourse, and/or to actively engage in the processes by which the rights and freedoms of individual citizens are shaped. Being called 'citizen' does not guarantee one's right to subjectivity, one's right to be heard or seen, nor one's right to attend school or participate in school life in relative safety.

Concluding Thoughts, Future Directions

As discussed, queer theories offer multiple ways to read how queer youth experience schooling. The promise of queer theories lay in the disruption of heteronormativity, in disclosing the power of naming, and in the possibilities embedded in a curricular understanding based on an embrace of partiality and fluidity. This disruption extends to assimilationist practices that fortify and reify nonfluid, unmoving constructions of queer youth, citizenship, and the teaching of queer issues.

A queered classroom politics is fluid and attentive to the needs of students, student activism, and their ideas of social change. It invites a reading of both the body and the space of classroom interactions, curricula, and pedagogies as ever changing. This is not to argue against individual student agency; however, agency is not linear, nor is it something that is bestowed from the teacher/instructor to the student body. There simply are no singularly epiphanal pedagogical moments through which to filter systemic change. Agency exists within the political space of the classroom in a recursive manner, which is evidenced by resistance both voiced and silent and through the many gradations of action and inaction.

There is much to be gained from a fluid curricular analysis of citizenship discourse, social justice pedagogy, and subsequent implications for the queer body. As Phelan argues, within the greater public imaginary many marginalized groups are understood to be, and are subsequently read as, "citizens." However, such a reading does not imply that all those publicly read as citizen are equal. However, as antiracist theories point out, racialized bodies, and nonnormative queer bodies must struggle against both silence and assimilation in order to be visible (Kumashiro, 2002). As a vital component of a reconceptualized classroom, queer theories and queer bodies offer multiple ways to re/read the language of inclusivity and dominant political norms. Reading these through citizenship reinforces the necessity of placing queer theories within a larger antioppression framework (which require interrogations of normalcy along myriad and intersecting identity constructions). Queer theories which view multiple identity constructions as part of an epistemological starting point, seek to address not only issues of homophobia, but also to challenge the myriad silences in which the normative foundations of heteronormative discourse are so deeply rooted.

We are arguing for a rereading of the school as a civic space, a queered space, as one where citizenship invites different ways of interpreting the queer body, and all bodies, in the classroom. Such an analysis demands an open rendering of both heteronormative and queer subjectivities. Too often a rush to inclusivity results in a reification of heteronormativity. The result is a discourse that, at best is inclusive through the categorical process of naming but does little to address underlying ideological constraints. A reformative classroom politics inclusive of the queer body would not only accord nonnormative bodies the same rights and freedoms of heteronormative bodies, but it would make visible the mechanisms of its subjection.

References

Berlant, L., & Warner, M. (1998). Sex in public. *Critical Inquiry,* 24, 547–566.
Butler, J. (1993a). *Bodies that matter: On the discursive limits of "sex."* New York: Routledge.

Butler, J. (1993b). Introduction, *Bodies that matter: On the discursive limits of "sex"* (pp. 1–23). New York: Routledge.

Crocco, M. S. (2001). The missing discourse about gender and sexuality in the social studies. *Theory Into Practice, 40*(1), 65–72.

Gay Lesbian and Straight Education Network. (2003). *The 2003 national school climate survey*. Washington, D.C.

Giffney, N. (2004). Denormatizing queer theory: More than (simply) lesbian and gay studies. *Feminist Theory, 5*(1), 73–78.

Giroux, H. (2003). Pedagogies of difference, race and representation: Film as a site of translation and politics. In P. P. Trifonas (Ed.), *Pedagogies of difference: Rethinking education for social change* (pp. 83–109). New York: RoutledgeFalmer.

Johnson, E. P. (2001). "Quare" studies or (almost) everything I know about queer studies I learned from my grandmother. *Text & Performance Quarterly, 21*, 1–25.

Kimmel, M. S. (2000). Masculinity as homophobia: Fear, shame and the silence in the construction of gender identity. In M. Adams, W. J. Blumenfeld, R. Castaneda, H. W. Hackman, Madeline L. Peteres & S. Zuniga (Eds.), *Readings for diversity and social justice: An Anthology on racism, sexism, anti-semitism, heterosexism, classism and ableism* (pp. 213–219). New York: Routledge.

Kumashiro, K. K. (2001). *Troubling intersections of race and sexuality: queer students of color and anti-oppressive education*. Lanham, MD: Rowman & Littlefield Publishers.

Kumashiro, K. K. (2002). *Troubling education: queer activism and antioppressive pedagogy*. New York: RoutledgeFalmer.

Lee, N., Murphy, D., & North, L. (1994). Sexuality, multicultural education, and the New York City public schools. *Radical Teacher, 45*, 12–16.

Loutzenheiser, L. W. (2001). *Painting outside the lines? Tensions and possibilities of alternative programs for marginalized students*. Unpublished Doctorial Dissertation, University of Wisconsin-Madison.

Loutzenheiser, L. W. (2002). Bein' seen and heard: Listening to young women in alternative schools. Anthropology and *Education Quarterly, 33*(4), 1–24.

Mac An Ghaill, M. (1993). *Making of men: Masculinities, sexualities and schooling*. Buckingham, UK: Open University Press.

MacIntosh, L. B. (2004). *Queering the body['s] politic: Gay-Straight alliances, citizenship and education*. University of British Columbia, Vancouver.

Pagenhart, P. (1994). The Very house of difference: Toward a more queerly defined multiculturalism. In L. Garber (Ed.), *Tilting the tower* (pp. 177–185). New York: Routledge.

Phelan, S. (2001). *Sexual strangers: gays, lesbians, and dilemmas of citizenship*. Philadelphia: Temple University Press.

Sumara, D., & Davis, B. (1999). Interrupting heteronormativity: Toward a queer curriculum theory. *Curriculum Inquiry, 29*(2), 191–208.

Talburt, S. (2000). *Subject to identity: Knowledge, sexuality and academic practices in higher education*. Albany, NY: State University of New York Press.

Thomas, C. (2000). Introduction: Identification, appropriation, proliferation. In C. Thomas (Ed.), *Straight with a twist: Queer theory and the subject of heterosexuality* (pp. 11–44). Urbana and Chicago: University of Illinois Press.

Turner, W. B. (2000). *A Genealogy of queer theory*. Philadelphia: Temple University Press.

Warner, M. (1993). Introduction. In M. Warner (Ed.), *Fear of a queer planet: Queer politics and social theory* (pp. vii–xxxi). Minneapolis: University of Minnesota Press.

Warner, M. (2002). *Publics and counterpublics*. New York: Zone Books.

William F. Pinar

FROM CHATTEL TO CITIZENRY: THE GENDER OF THE LAW IN THE SEXUAL POLITICS OF RACE

> [T]he transformation from chattel to citizenry is mediated through a complicated process of sexualization and engendering.
> ROBYN WIEGMAN (1993, p. 446)

One hundred years ago, lynching was "America's National Crime" (Wells-Barnett, 1977/1901, p. 30). The centrality of castration to the lynching event underscores that racial politics and violence in the United States have been—and still are—simultaneously a sexual politics. (The widespread white rape of black female slaves established the fact that racial domination is sexualized.) The gendered character of the law in the U.S. and the sexualized nature of racial violence conflated in early twentieth-century debates in the U.S. Congress over antilynching legislation. By juxtaposing Michael Grossberg's study of the gender of U.S. law with Claudine Ferrell's study of antilynching legislation efforts, I suggest that U.S. citizenship is a gendered and racialized concept. How can we dedicate ourselves to "educating citizens in a multicultural society" (Banks 1997) when the very category of the civic is saturated with the sexual and the racialized?

The Gender of the Law

Masculinity spoke loudly but not with a single voice from the bench and bar.
(MICHAEL GROSSBERG 1990, 147)

Above all, lynching is about the law.
(ROBYN WIEGMAN 1993, 445)

Especially during the nineteenth and early twentieth centuries, law was not just another profession; it was a distinctively gendered one. Embedded in American legal consciousness, Michael Grossberg (1990) argues, has been the notion that the bar is a masculine domain. That is less so today, but for much of the history of the American bar "masculinity was so fundamental to the profession's consciousness that . . . it acted as an unarticulated first principle" (Grossberg 1990, p. 134). By examining what Grossberg (p. 134) terms the "institutionalization of masculinity in the bar," we can glimpse links between the public and private sides of men's lives in nineteenth-century and early twentieth-century America, gendered sides that became racialized in the congressional struggles over antilynching legislation.

After the Revolutionary War, Grossberg tells us, lawyers occupied a powerful position in the new nation, suggested in part by their rapidly increasing numbers. Those practicing law increased almost four times as fast as the population. The United States became a "lawyer-ridden nation" (Grossberg, 1990, p. 134). Especially in the South lawyers comprised a significant percentage of state legislators who had won wealth and respect through their profession. As the number of men practicing the profession increased, so did the sense that the lawyer's job was a masculine one. As a masculinist and homosocial community, the bar influenced how lawyers performed institutional roles and formulated public policies (Grossberg, 1990).

The profession's distinctive institutionalization of masculinity took shape in the opening decades of the nineteenth century. Grossberg points to a gradual disjunction between law and literature that illustrates how masculinity helped shape the bar's professional consciousness. In colonial America, the law had been a sideline for merchants, farmers, and planters. Lawyers were assumed to be men of letters broadly educated and conversant in all branches of knowledge. As practitioners of an ancient and learned profession, these men were assumed to be wordsmiths, skilled at composing not only legal briefs, but philosophical essays, political satire, even fiction. During the revolutionary era, though, this marriage between law and letters began to dissolve as lawyers took up new professional roles. As the full-time professional replaced the part-time amateur, literary pursuits (specifically novels and poetry) were no longer perceived as appropriate lawyerly avocations (Grossberg, 1990).

Increasingly a man's admission to the bar and his subsequent professional success depended on his conformity with dominant masculine values. These values are suggested in the obituaries of antebellum lawyers, who tended to be characterized as "fearless," "manly," and "independent" (quoted in Grossberg 1990, p. 138). These qualities represented a lawyerly version of what Grossberg (p. 138) terms "responsible manhood." It was a time of unprecedented opportunity for American (white) men, and for unprecedented failure, captured in the image of drunken husbands guzzling family wages in dimly lit barrooms. Lawyers themselves aggressively promoted the image of the lawyer as carefully reasoning his way—"our" way—through complex and momentous problems, soberly addressing the complexities of political life, courageously defending the victimized in court, and acting as an independent crusader for moral right in society (Grossberg 1990).

Women's challenges to the bar intensified the profession's engendering. In the last decades of the century a few women demanded a place in the masculine and homosocial community of lawyers. Barred from the profession by custom and statute, women were forced to mount campaigns in order to receive a legal education. They lobbied legislators and filed suits, on occasion with success. "Their challenge," Grossberg (1990, p. 145) tells us, "stirred a particularly telling mixture of resistance and support that adds another perspective on the role of masculinity in defining the nineteenth-century legal community."

The general reaction of practicing male lawyers to the prospect of female colleagues appears to have been one of disbelief, punctuated at times with "horror and disgust." Many male legislators, judges, and lawyers echoed the views of a California lawmaker who spoke against a bill that would end gender bias in the legal profession: "The sphere of women is infinitely more important than that of men, and that sphere is the home" (quoted in Grossberg, 1990, p. 145). When Wisconsin Chief Justice Edward Ryan denied Lavinia Goodell the right to practice law, he felt compelled to remind her of proper gender roles: "[N]ature has tempered women as little for the juridical conflicts of the courtroom," he explained, "as for the physical conflicts of the battlefield" (quoted in Grossberg, 1990, p. 145). Ryan was sure that the use of masculine pronouns in statutes regulating the bar communicated a legislative intent to limit the bar to men (Grossberg, 1990).

In fact, the Chief Justice rejected the very possibility of reading "persons" in a gender-free fashion: "If we should follow that authority in ignoring the distinction of sex, we do not perceive why it should not emasculate the constitution itself and include females in the constitutional right of male suffrage and male qualification. Such a rule would be one of judicial revolution, not of judicial construction" (quoted passages in Grossberg, 1990, p. 146). Judges like Ryan reproduced the ideology of "separate spheres" (see, for instance, Haynes, 1997) by restating it jurisprudentially. The legal statutes they interpreted were presumably indeterminate and flexible, but their interpretations were hardly declarations of fixed rules. They were expressions of the bar's fantasies of responsible manhood (Grossberg, 1990).

In 1880 there were exactly 75 female lawyers; thirty years later, despite the proliferation of women's colleges and the women's rights movement, there were only 1,341. Some states still forbade women to practice law; scores of the leading law schools excluded them from studying law (Filene, 1998). Only slowly were women admitted to the bar. Their presence resulted in the creation of a female sphere in the law as part of the profession's new hierarchy; it did not change its gendered disposition. Within that separate sphere women created alternative professional institutions, among them the Woman's International Bar Association, founded in 1888, the Equite Club, a correspondence club of women lawyers also founded in the 1880s, and the *Women Lawyers Journal*, established in 1911 (Grossberg, 1990).

For women, as for *ethnic* and black men, prejudice plus legal specialization resulted in professional segregation. While male Jewish lawyers found themselves restricted to criminal work and personal-injury cases, women found themselves kept out of the courtroom, restricted to processing paperwork, working in secretarial pools, and doing research at libraries (Grossberg, 1990). Yet the presence of women in the legal community, like that of ethnics, blacks, and lower-class whites, provoked professional battles and debates that would eventually change the American legal profession. But not immediately: when a woman challenged her exclusion from Hastings College of Law by pointing out that an Asian student had been accepted, the lawyer representing the California school retorted that "the Chinaman" had been thrown out too (quoted in Grossberg, 1990, p. 149).

Not all professions were closed to women, of course. During the late nineteenth century, teaching was increasingly feminized, while remaining "pedagogy for patriarchy" (Grumet, 1988; Tyack and Hansot, 1990). Medicine, too, provides a gendered contrast to the bar. The barriers to a medical career, though several, were less impassable than those blocking women's entry to the bar. Barbara Harris (quoted in Grossberg, 1990, p. 149) notes: "Female doctors could claim that their careers were natural extensions of women's nurturant, healing role in the home and that they protected feminine modesty by ministering to members of their own sex. By contrast, women lawyers were clearly intruding on the public domain explicitly reserved for men."

The early nineteenth-century bar had been strictly a man's profession. Manhood and, later, masculinity (see Bederman, 1995) were profoundly embedded in lawyers' professional consciousness and community membership. Patriarchal values helped position the lawyer politically in American society and legitimated his power by making it appear natural, if not preordained. Because judges and lawyers operated in a relatively autonomous professional realm, their versions of responsible manhood became "law." As Grossberg (1990, p. 151) concludes, "Institutionalized masculinity had become part of American legal consciousness." In becoming so, the law, even well into the twentieth century, was a man's world, and exchanges within the law enforcement and law-making must be understood as exchanges in a male homosocial economy. It was a man's world that was being constructed and enforced, and struggles over legal issues, in Congress over constitutionality, were also struggles among men over the nature of manhood. As we will see in the following section, U.S. congressmen—white men, almost all of them—used legalistic issues, such as "states rights" and "constitutionality" to wage war over white men's right of access to black men's bodies.

"[A] Very Important Prerogative Reserved for the States" (quoted in Ferrell 1986, 5)

> [C]astration is also an inverted sexual encounter between black men and white men.
> (ROBYN WIEGMAN, 1993, p. 458 n.)

In 1961, in response to right-wing warnings that federal civil rights legislation would fail to legislate morality, Martin Luther King, Jr. asserted that, "the law may not be able to make a man love me, but it can keep him from lynching me" (quoted in Ferrell 1986, p. 1). Forty years earlier, "the law" did not even try to keep white men from lynching black men. During 1917 and 1918, while three hundred thousand black soldiers served their country, a tenth of them in Europe, at home white men mutilated (often castrating) some one hundred young black men. The contradiction between American idealism and the daily reality of lynching became intolerable for many who became more determined than ever that the federal government must be made to intervene in the "peculiar" practice (Ferrell, 1986).

Along with its friends, allies, and a handful of northern congressmen, the NAACP* refused to accept the indifference with which most Americans regarded the practice of lynching (Zangrando, 1980). Reformulating their earlier antilynching strategies in the face of resistant states and localities and rejecting the unspoken but widespread belief that racial justice and constitutional federalism were mutually exclusive, a coalition of mostly black and white men began a thirty-year effort to persuade Congress to pass antilynching legislation. Although they never succeeded, national indifference to lynching slowly changed, as did the crime for which the antilynchers wanted federal intervention. Not until 1952 did the United States record its first lynch-free year. By the 1950s lynching was no longer a national issue, but by 1950 no longer did the federal government imagine itself unable to do what the states had long refused to do, namely, try to protect black men from white (Ferrell, 1986).

Southerners may have lost the argument for "states rights" during the first half of the nineteenth century, but they won during the second half, and the first half of the twentieth century as well. Northerners who were once willing to fight and die to preserve "the Union" seemed, after their military victory, quite willing to concede the point, seduced by doctrines of "federalism," especially when "race" was concerned. Northern capitulation to southern arguments for "state rights" and federalism was so complete that on occasion certain southern congressmen actually referred to an "inalienable right" to lynching (Ferrell, 1986). The Emancipation Proclamation was just that (see Hartman, 1997), and rhetoric it would remain, as reformer Archibald Grimké put it, a "national contradiction between profession and practice, promise and performance" (quoted in Ferrell, 1986, p. 4).

---

*Editor's note: National Association for the Advancement of Colored People, formed in 1909, is one of the oldest civil rights organizations in the United States.

In December 1921, only days before the House of Representatives turned its attention to the Dyer antilynching bill, the Greensboro (N.C.) *Daily News* characterized the measure as "[a]nother invasion of State's rights by the Federal government; but the Federal Government is justified in this instance, because none of the States had made an honest effort to prevent lynchings by making examples of those who indulge in them" (quoted in Ferrell, 1986, p. 5). In contrast, the *Nashville* (Tennessee) *Banner* informed its readers that: "[t]his anti-lynching law would overthrow a very important prerogative reserved for the states, and would be a dangerous encroachment on the right of local self-government—the principle of federation, the groundwork on which the Union is built" (quoted in Ferrell, 1986, p. 5). Odd to hear the grandchildren of Confederate soldiers speaking about "the groundwork on which the Union is built," but in the context of debate over antilynching legislation, the "union" to which they referred was a sexually violent one between white men and black (Wiegman, 1993).

Not only southerners were involved in the ruse. Democrat Clarence Lea of California, for instance, declared that the Dyer bill was not only unconstitutional, it would convert the federal government into "a colossus with a club over the State," asserting "the superior virtue of a superman" and dictating "standards of virtue." Republican Edward C. Little of Kansas City was not seduced by the gendered fears of his California colleague. The Dyer bill was quite constitutional, although he did allow, dryly, that measure would deprive the states of "the alleged power . . . of allowing their citizens to burn people occasionally without any interference by the Federal Government" (quoted in Ferrell, 1986, p. 6). The rather concrete issue of white men sexually mutilating black men's bodies was abstracted into a constitutional question of states' rights and the role of the federal government in local affairs. While not doubting the sincerity of some of those who participated in these debates, it is difficult to believe that these white men had a clue regarding the sexual subtext of what they were saying.

However much they relied on constitutional arguments, southerners were never content with them. Sooner or later God would have to be brought in, as when Florida Representative Frank Clark explained to Congress in 1908:

> If God Almighty had intended these two races to be equal, He would have so created them. He made the Caucasian of handsome figure, straight hair, regular features, high brow, and superior intelligence. He created the negro, giving him a black skin, kinky hair, thick lips, flat nose, low brow, low order of intelligence, and repulsive features. I do not believe that these differences were the result of either accident or mistake on the part of the Creator. I believe He knew what He was doing, and I believe He did just what He wanted to do." (quoted in Ferrell, 1986, p. 82)

Others saw "race relations" more, well, erotically. Extolled as "the architect of environmentalism in American education" (Pinar et al., 1995, p. 104), Lester Frank Ward was sure that something instinctive moved the black man "to seek a higher race with which to mate" (Ferrell, 1986, p. 85). Of course, this was sociologically speaking, only. While some believed interracial mating was conceivable (others argued that fertile offspring could not be produced by such unions), it was still "unnatural." After all, white men explained, "the black penis [is] too large for the white woman's uterine canal and the mulatto children produced [are] mentally superior but physically inferior to the Negro" (quoted in Ferrell, 1986, p. 85). One must not tamper with the black body, unless of course that body be male and had, presumably, entered the body of a white female. Then, as southern apologist Winfield Collins "explained" after World War I: "As the world is to be made safe for democracy, so ought the South to be made safe for white women" (quoted in Ferrell, 1986, p. 86). To fight that war required lynching, white men insisted. Lynching was, Washington University historian Roland G. Usher explained in 1919, "nothing more nor less than the old self-help" (quoted in Ferrell, 1986, p. 87). Lynching was not a violation of the law; it was, white men insisted, its execution (Ferrell, 1986).

Beginning with the great antilynching crusader Ida B. Wells in the final quarter of the nineteenth century and continuing in the twentieth-century with the NAACP, African Americans fought the sexualized mutilations of black male and, on occasion, female bodies. The high points of the legislative campaign occurred from 1918 to 1923, 1934 to 1940, and 1946 to 1950. The U.S. House of Representatives passed the measure in 1922, 1937, and 1940, but the Senate—dominated by southerners, conservatives, white men—declined to even vote on the measure. This recalcitrance underscores the centrality of lynching to the American civic experience, "an almost integral part of our national folkways" as Walter White (1929, p. viii) characterized it in *Rope and Faggot*. It was "America's national crime," as Ida B. Wells well understood (1977/1901, p. 30). Many African Americans knew that lynching was no eccentric southern distraction from the main problems of racial justice in the United States. Understanding lynching and white citizens' legal protection of it are key to understanding the problem of "race" in America (Zangrando, 1980).

The political struggle against lynching always took a back seat to "larger" public imperatives, such as the GOP's legislative agenda for 1922–1923, the New Deal's economic initiatives in 1937 and 1938, and those Cold War issues with which Washington politicians became obsessed by the late 1940s. Regionally, the Commission on Interracial Cooperation of the 1920s and the Association of Southern Women for the Prevention of Lynching throughout the 1930s, seemed, finally, more concerned about their white neighbors' sensibilities and sectional autonomy than about the bodies of black men. The modernizing influences of federal interventions, such as the Tennessee Valley Authority, undermined only slightly southern loyalties to states' rights and regionalism. In the 1940s, anti-Communist hysteria as well as their own hesitations slowed reformers associated with the Southern Conference for Human Welfare and the Southern Regional Council (Zangrando, 1980). As late as 1955, fourteen-year old Emmett Till would be mutilated for whistling at a white woman, his severed penis stuffed in his mouth (see Alexander 1994, p. 102).

Conclusion: "Homosexual Panic, Latent Energy and "[t]he Political Unconscious of White Masculinity" (Kobena Mercer, 1994, p. 188)

> *[T]he speaking subject is also the subject about which it speaks.*
> (MICHEL FOUCAULT, 1987, p. 10)

The still shocking refusal of white men to enact federal legislation to criminalize lynching underscores how powerful a symbol lynching was. As they had for a century (and continue to do so today), white southern men led the reactionary refusal to protect the civil rights of all Americans, disingenuously crying "constitutionality" and "states rights" to prevent federal intervention in southern barbarism. A masculinized symbol system par excellence, law and legislation constituted symbolizations of disavowed and racialized male-male desire (Hocquenghem, 1978; Grossberg, 1990). Southern white men were not about to keep other southern white men away from the bodies of young black men.

These racialized sexual dynamics—camouflaged in Congress by abstract argumentation over God, country, and states' rights—desublimated in late twentieth-century U.S. prisons, where gangs of heterosexually identified black men bypassed sexually available white and black gay prisoners to rape and "turn-out"—convert to "punks"—straight, preferably heterosexual-married, young white men (see Pinar, 2001, Chapters 16 and 17). In late twentieth-century U.S. prisons, the (homo)sexual politics of race became unmistakable.

The sexual politics of "race"—rendered vivid and horrific in the history of lynching and citizens' struggles against it—need to be studied (McClintock 1971) across the curriculum, especially in the social studies. As curriculum theorists have insisted, knowledge is, however, not enough (see Britzman, 1998). Simply informing students hardly guarantees their thoughtful and engaged civic participation in the racialized public sphere that is "America."* Knowledge guarantees nothing except the end of ignorance.

That *is* something, however. There will be those who will be moved by the facts. Ida B. Wells (1969/1892, p. 101) knew the power of knowledge: "The very frequent inquiry made after my lectures by interested friends is, 'What can I do to help the cause?' The answer always is, 'Tell the world the facts.' When the Christian world knows the alarming growth and extent of outlawry in our land, some means will be found to stop it." Wells soon came to realize she had overestimated the moral righteousness of the "Christian world," but she never lost faith in telling the truth. Nor must we.

---

*Editor's note: Or in Canada, as well. In that country, the sexual politics of "race" is evident in the treatment of aboriginal peoples and events such as the World War II refusal of Jewish immigration and Canadian internment of citizens of Japanese ancestry.

References

Alexander, E. (1994). "Can you be BLACK and look at this?": Reading the Rodney King video(s), in Thelma Golden (Ed.), *Black male: Representations of masculinity in contemporary American art*, pp. 91–110. New York: Whitney Museum of American Art. (Harry N. Abrams, Inc.).

Banks, J. A. (1997). *Educating citizens in a multicultural society*. New York: Teachers College Press.

Bederman, G. (1995). *Manliness and civilization: A cultural history of gender and race in the United States, 1880–1917*. Chicago: University of Chicago Press.

Britzman, D. P. (1998). *Lost subjects, contested objects: Toward a psychoanalytic inquiry of learning*. Albany: State University of New York Press.

Ferrell, C. L. (1986). *Nightmare and dream: Antilynching in Congress, 1917–1922*. New York: Garland.

Filene, P. G.(1998). *Him/her/self*. [3rd edition; 1st edition published in 1974 by Harcourt, Brace, Jovanovich.] Baltimore, MD: Johns Hopkins University Press.

Foucault, M. (1987). Maurice Blanchot: The thought from outside, in *Foucault/Blanchot*, B. Mussumi (Trans.), pp. 7–58. New York: Zone Books.

Grossberg, M. (1990). Institutionalizing masculinity: The law as a masculine profession, in Mark C. Carnes & Clyde Griffen (Eds.), *Meanings for manhood: Constructions of masculinity in Victorian America*, pp. 133–151. Chicago: University of Chicago Press.

Grumet, M. R. (1988). *Bitter milk: Women and teaching*. Amherst: University of Massachusetts Press.

Harris, B. (1978). *Beyond her sphere: Women and the professions in American history*. Westport, CT: Greenwood.

Hartman, S. V. (1997). *Scenes of subjection: Terror, slavery, and self-making in nineteenth century America*. New York: Oxford University Press.

Haynes, C. A. (1998*). Divine destiny: Gender and race in nineteenth-century protestantism*. Jackson: University Press of Mississippi.

Mercer, K. (1994). *Welcome to the jungle: New positions in black cultural studies*. New York: Routledge.

Pinar, W. F. (2001). *The gender of racial politics and violence in America*. New York: Peter Lang.

Pinar, W. F., Reynolds, W. M., Slattery, P., & Taubman, P. M. (1995). *Understanding curriculum: An introduction to historical and contemporary curriculum discourses*. New York: Peter Lang.

Tyack, D., & Hansot, E. (1990). *Learning together: A history of coeducation in American schools*. New Haven, CT: Yale University Press.

Wells, Ida B. (1969). *A red record. Tabulated statistics and alleged causes of lynchings in the United States, 1892–1893–1894*, in *On lynchings*, pp. 22–34. [Preface by August Meier.] New York: Arno Press/New York Times. (original published 1892).

Wells-Barnett, Ida B. & Addams, J. (1977). Lynching and the excuse for it/Respect for law, in J. Addams and I. B. Wells, *Lynching and Rape: An Exchange of Views*, pp. 28–34. (original published 1901). [Edited, and with an introduction, by Bettina Aptheker.] Chicago: University of Illinois, Occasional Paper No. 25.

White, W. (1929). *Rope and faggot: A biography of Judge Lynch*. New York: Alfred A. Knopf.

Wiegman, Robyn (1993, January). The anatomy of lynching. *Journal of the History of Sexuality* 3 (3), 445–467.

Zangrando, Robert L. (1980). *The NAACP Crusade against lynching, 1909–1950*. Philadelphia: Temple University Press.

IV

TROUBLING VISIONS OF CITIZENSHIP EDUCATION

David W. Blades and George H. Richardson

RESTARTING THE INTERRUPTED DISCOURSE OF THE PUBLIC GOOD: GLOBAL CITIZENSHIP EDUCATION AS MORAL IMPERATIVE

The Moral Imperative of World Citizenship Education

"Why become a global citizen? Why care about the planet? Ultimately one of the reasons is because when we learn to live and work together, we preserve humanity. I think humanity is worth preserving." (Matt, a 10th-grade student)

The legacy of the 20th century may well be the irrevocable effects of scientific development and rapid technological innovation on human existence. Inventions such as automobiles, antibiotics, television, nuclear energy, and jet airline travel and developments in fields such as genetics and the Internet have come to profoundly affect the way we see ourselves and live with each other in our local communities, nation states, and the world. As a former Secretary-General of the United Nations observed:

> We are now living in the era of the global society. Which means a world where those who act are not just States, but also non-governmental organizations, national parliaments, private companies, the media, associations of all sorts, academics, intellectuals, and each and every man and woman who feels he or she is a full member of the big human family. (Boutros-Ghali, 1996, p. 2)

This sense of family is disturbed, however, by the concomitant realization that the modern scientific and technological innovations of the 20th century have also created problems that urgently demand a global response. In his overview of the state of the world as we moved into the 21st century, Brown (2000) observed that human civilization faces well-entrenched practices that may compromise our future, such as the industrial production of carbon dioxide, depletion of water tables from irrigation, shrinking cropland through urbanization, worldwide deforestation, and loss of biodiversity through human-induced extinction. At the same time, rapid technological innovations in the areas such as human cloning and the production of androids are forcing ethical and moral issues that require immediate public attention (Richardson & Blades, 2001; Blades, 1999; Kumano, 1994). But humankind already faces pandemics of AIDS and tuberculosis, regions of chronic conflict, waste from obsolete nuclear weapons, and unpredictable financial markets—to name only a few issues on our present agenda. Indeed, this century may well prove to be crucial in our history; we will either make substantive and lasting changes to the way we live with each other and our planet or this century could be our last (Blades, 2000; Bright, 2000; Leslie, 1996; Orr, 1992).

One location of hope amidst this challenge to human survival is the 20th century phenomenon of the worldwide establishment and development of systems of public education. This development presents the possibility of global school curricula that enable students in every culture to gain the knowledge, courage, and ability needed to begin to address the issues they face and will face as global citizens.

Developing curriculum of world citizenship will not be easy, but it is essential to human survival. Given the highly complex matrix of public policy issues that are transnational in scope, developing a curriculum of world citizenship is a moral imperative since it supports the metaethical principle of human survival. This principle represents an acknowledgment that, as humans, we are fully complicit in the life of the planet since the survival of many species on the earth is inseparable from our survival. Given our ability to make conscious choices and create technologies, humanity has a particular moral obligation to act in such a way that we widen the imaginative space of the public sphere to encourage the development of what Hannah Arendt (1968) calls an ethic of "care for the world." Such an ethic calls us to acknowledge and protect the Other as an inherent aspect of our humanity. As Emmanuel Levinas (1985) noted, "it is I who support the Other and am responsible for him. . . . Responsibility is what is incumbent on me exclusively and what *humanly*, I cannot refuse (p. 114).

Reimagining Education for World Citizenship

> "It [a breakthrough on global issues] might not be seen as an immediate effect, but I believe those students will aim for it when becoming adult and they can solve them, so I think it's a good idea to discuss with them together and see what happens." (Takumi, a 10th grade student on why an international dialogue with other students on global issues is important)

"If we could find some kind of mutual agreement on what we think needs to be fixed with the world, then maybe we could actually accomplish something." (Kyla, a 10th-grade student)

Imagine students in secondary schools around the world engaged in social action that directly deals with the environmental and technological issues facing humankind. Realizing this possibility would first require opportunities for students to engage in dialogue with their peers in order to view issues from other perspectives. Arendt (1968) calls such a conversation "learning to imagine the other," noting that

> The more people's standpoints I have in my mind while I am pondering a given issue, and the better I can imagine how I would feel and think if I were in their place, the stronger my capacity for representative thinking and the more valid my final conclusions, my opinion. (p. 241)

However, such conversations do not develop in isolation of the discourses that form and inform globalization. An integral feature of globalization today, observes philosopher Mark Kingwell, is a "consumerist arms race" where, "ever in search of a competitive advantage or pocket of enviable happiness, we are now driven to newer and more inventive forms of acquisition" (2000, p. 215). The result is a *de facto* limitation of imagination in the public sphere to a rationale of consumerism that supports global systems that are dependent on fossil fuels, willing to exploit cheap labor and tolerant of destructive environmental practices. What is urgently needed is a shift towards reclaiming our civic responsibility as inhabitants of the earth: A global citizenship. Central to this new direction is the moral imperative to, in the words of Zygmund Bauman, "restart . . . the interrupted discourse of the common good" (Bauman, 1999, p. 107).

Conceptions of a common good that inform and direct our relations with each other and how we might live together begin, suggests Smith (1999), with the formation of a *global imaginary*. As Smith notes, such an imaginary "pertains less to any characteristic of the world in its ordinary condition than to what certain people *imagine* that condition to be" (pp. 3–4). Finding this imagination is also a curriculum project since schools are ideally situated as locations for initiating a worldwide discourse on the common good. We advance that as we begin our sojourn through the 21st century, humankind thus needs a *curricular imaginary* of global citizenship that might initiate and build a discourse of the common good.

Contemporary civic education practices are unequal to developing the kind of curricular imaginary we are suggesting for two reasons. First, thought of in traditional, reproductive terms as "a way to stabilize a normative conception of a nation and its instrument of governing, the state" (Feinberg, 2001, p. 203), civic education has shown itself unable to engage students in grappling with the dilemmas and issues that confront them in their daily lives. As bound to the national structure of parliaments, parties, regular elections, and patriotism, citizenship education is increasingly circumscribed and made irrelevant by extranational organizations such as the G-8, the WTO, and the World Bank (Richardson, 2004).

Second, constrained by a results-based, high-stakes testing environment that dramatically confines the space for imagination, conversation, and action on one hand, and framed by neoliberal conceptions of citizenship that privilege individual rights over communal and collective responsibilities on the other, citizenship education has effectively abandoned the notion of the public sphere and the common good (Apple, 1998; Richardson & Blades, 2001). The net result of these practices has been to render much of contemporary civic education bereft of moral purpose and fundamentally inconsequential to the lives of students.

Reclaiming the discourses of globalization in order to build a common good is not a naïve seduction to the idealistic premise that a common good preexists in some sense. What we imagine possible is a worldwide generative curriculum where global citizenship becomes a way of being rather than merely a way of knowing. When we conceive of global citizenship in ontological terms we become aware that we live in a "complex network of mutually dependent places and groups, within, but more important, beyond the borders of nations" (Parker, Grossman, Kubow, Kurth-Schai & Nakayama, 1998, p. 136). And as philosopher Martha Nussbaum (1997) remarks, people who have developed the imaginative capacity to project their citizenship beyond the nation project their humanity along the same trajectory. Such people, she notes, "see themselves not simply as citizens of some local region or group, but also, and above all, as human beings bound to all other human beings by ties of recognition and concern" (p. 10).

Revealing Possibilities for World Citizenship: The JASPER Project

We believe that the platform for developing the ontology of global citizenship may already exist, in a limited form, among secondary school students. In 2001, we formed the Japan-Alberta Science/Social Studies Project for Educational Reform (JASPER), a long-term educational research project designed to bring together students, teachers, and academics in Shizuoka Prefecture in Japan and in the Canadian province of Alberta so that they may examine contemporary issues that require an understanding of the responsibilities of world citizenship.

The first part of the JASPER Project involved engaging secondary school students (n=194) in conversation through questionnaires, written responses to statements, and special forums about how they understand and imagine their responsibilities as active, responsible world citizens (Richardson, G., et al., 2003). Our meetings with these high school students revealed that despite cultural and linguistic differences, they share very common attitudes and concerns about global issues and their responsibility as citizens of the world. For example, over 90% of the students in each country agree with the statement, "During this century it will be more important to understand the responsibilities of being an active and responsible member of the world community than being a member of a particular country." Students were also in agreement that the most important issues facing humankind are related to environmental degradation and the exact same percentage of students in both countries identified global warming as the single most important environmental issue facing humankind.

Students in both countries expressed very similar reservations about the benefits of science and technology. As one Japanese student observed, "while science enriched our lives, it [also] destroyed the earth resulting in that human beings are well off but poor in mentality." This sentiment was echoed by a Canadian student who noted, "although science and technology have made the world a better place for humans, it [sic] has taken a toll on the environment. Technology could be beneficial, but we have reached a point where we are only competing to make faster cars and more product than to improve the environment." When asked to explain why they might disagree that science and technology have made the world a better place, both groups identified environmental problems introduced through technological innovation (such as exhaust from automobiles) as their primary concern.

Such results are not surprising given that these students live in countries of relative wealth and have ready access to media such as television; we suspect students in most industrialized countries would provide similar responses to our questions. What was significant from our conversations was the evidence of an emergent sense of global citizenship among these students, independent of nationality. Over 90% of the students agree that in the 21st century it is more important to understand the responsibilities of being an active and responsible member of the world community rather than being a member of a particular country. This agreement became nearly unanimous when asked about whether they will need to work with students in other countries to solve issues such as global warming. Students strongly maintain that to learn to be active, responsible members of the world community, they will need to have conversations with their peers in other countries about world issues. As one student commented, "I think diversity, in general, is essential to the human population. You could solve a lot more problems with different perspectives than just everybody of the same perspective." A student noted the value of international dialogue around global issues observing, "I think it's a good idea. We can understand and examine the different ideas through discussion with foreign students," adding the critical comment, "we tend to have a biased idea when talking among Japanese friends."

While student voices confirmed our belief in the value of international partnerships among students to deal with global issues, their comments also suggest the ontological nature of global citizenship. It was clear in our conversations that students are willing to reclaim the discourse on a global public good but on *their* terms and in ways that surprised us. For example, students in both countries challenged our idea of a conversation *only* between Canadian and Japanese students. Acknowledging the potential influence of the two countries, students nevertheless reminded us that citizenship must involve a moral obligation to helping the material conditions of citizens in less developed nations. As one student commented,

I'd rather like to talk with the students from the developing countries. Since we live in developed countries, we have an advantage to talk about robots and medical systems. We have longer life, and can easily take medication. There is a big difference in prosperity. Meanwhile, there are many people who have to die from starvation. I'd like to talk with the same generation from those countries.

Students also commented that while international conversations can help identify world issues, action on these issues need to begin in their own countries. "As much as I would like for borders not to be a concern to people," commented one student, "they really are still . . . countries need to take their own stance and decide how they are going to deal with these problems within the country before we can bring it to an international level." In response, another student added, "As much as it is one world, it's filled with diverse economies and people that can't live by one rule."

The sophistication of student comments about actually addressing world issues reminded us that developing a global imaginary must include the voices of this generation. These voices, when invited to participate in public discourse on the common good, interrupt received or preexisting notions of global citizenship, whether from those concerned to direct students to social action on particular global issues or to the default existing discourse of consumerism. For example, one student displayed a healthy skepticism about the objectivity of the "truths" he had learned in civic classes noting, "the correctness of information is quite doubtful. Information could be operated and even fiction produced by someone. It is a reality that each individual convey what they think, not believing in the information given." Students also emphasized that citizenship education must be more than conversation. As one student reminded us, "learning and experiencing citizenship are two different things. We can't keep just learning about it and thinking about [it]. We actually have to get out there and do it." The interruption of such student voices demonstrates that citizenship is a forever-emergent ontology, brought forth continually as the children who inherit the world are allowed to contribute in words and action to what it means to be a citizen of the world.

Imagining the *Agora* as a Space of Global Civic Engagement

"I haven't experienced this globe enough to comprehend what would happen if I didn't change my actions. That's another reason it's important to talk to people in other countries. If anything, it's just this beautiful forum where you have the opportunity to share your collective experience." (Ava, a 10th-grade student)

Globalization has what David G. Smith terms an undeniable "facticity" (Smith, 1999). Put more directly, it is an already existing discourse with a tangible series of effects ranging from unregulated, worldwide flows of capital to deforestation on a planetary scale. However, if there are few questions about the "fact" of globalization, there are significant questions about whether a parallel civic discourse has emerged that provides us with the moral grounding to act as global citizens. Viewing this disjunction, political philosopher Will Kymlicka has concluded, "globalization is undoubtedly producing a new civil society, but it has not yet produced anything we can recognize as transnational democratic citizenship" (Kymlicka, 2001, p. 326).

Thus, in the face of what Anthony Giddens terms the "democratic deficit" "between [nations] and the global forces that affect the lives of their citizens" (Giddens, 2000, p. 34), there is an urgent need to create a space where it is possible for schools to "return to the political" (Mouffe, 1993) on a global scale. If we accept the need for such a return, the question emerges of how and in what form it should emerge. We suggest one way to develop this discourse might be through the metaphor of the *Agora*—both a call to civic engagement and a place where engagement is fostered.

In classical Greece the two poles of daily life were divided between the explicitly public, the *Ekklesia*, or public assembly and the explicitly private, the *Oikos*, or private household. But between these two lay the Agora—or marketplace, a site where public and private spheres intersected. In Zygmund Bauman's terms, the Agora was a space of "communication" not keeping the private and public spheres apart, but instead "assuring a smooth and constant traffic between them" (Bauman, 1999, p. 87). It was this communicative flow that Bauman asserts was essential to the maintenance of the *polis* as a democratic entity.

The metaphor of the Agora is one that allows us to take up Bauman's explicit challenge to act on the moral imperative to restart a public discourse on the common good. But as Alistair McIntyre reminds us, such a discourse is more than a theoretical exchange: "We learn what our common good is, and indeed, what our own individual goods are, not primarily and never only by theoretical reflection, but in everyday shared activities, and the evaluation of alternatives that those activities impose" (MacIntyre, 1999, pp. 135–136). These "everyday shared activities" are best engaged through the creation of a shared location where the daily commerce of living informs the marketplace of political discourse. Bauman and MacIntyre's ideas are echoed in those of curriculum theorist Jon Nixon who asks: "How can we constitute and revivify this sphere as a place of genuine *communication* in which pluralities of difference are recognized and empowered?" (Nixon, 2001, p. 223, italics in text).

In response to Nixon's question, we believe that the conversations we held with high school students in Japan and Canada in the JASPER Project demonstrate that it is possible to think in terms of creating an international Agora, whether in virtual form, through direct, face-to-face interaction, or some kind of hybrid of the two.

Such a meeting place could begin as other countries invest in such international, interdisciplinary partnerships between classrooms. Imagine placing secondary school Social Studies and Science education—or their equivalents—at the same time in a school timetable. Cooperating teachers in the two subject area disciplines could develop their courses towards integrating around a particular global issue, such as global warming (Richardson & Blades, 2001). Teachers involved in the JASPER project believe that the science and societal aspects of this issue would naturally transfer between classes, creating a dynamic and deep conversation on the issue. Now imagine such a conversation conducted with a partner classroom in another country. One Japanese student called this possibility a "fine collision" of ideas; his Canadian peers agree, arguing, "two diverse minds are better than two minds that think alike." The initial results of the JASPER Project suggest such an initiative is easily accomplished and based on our conversation with high school students in both countries we predict that the conversations in the Agora would soon move students to take up social action as members of their home countries and as members of the world community. As one student commented, "There's more things we could be doing. In school we just get a general overview of what we could do. But we really don't try any of it out or learn as much as we probably could."

It is particularly in providing a space for students' voices to come to us as emergent, interruptive democratic narratives filled with moral purpose that the Agora can assume its full potential. As a global marketplace of ideas where discussions of the common good are not removed from the commerce of everyday living, and as the meeting ground between students' more private, national selves and the institutionalized public discourse of globalization, the Agora can insert itself into the civic life of the global community as an essential site of communication and empowerment between the public and private spheres. As Jenna, a 10th grade student reminds us, "Yes it's a really big jump to think of ourselves as just a citizen of a city to a citizen of the world, but in reality we're all born of the same thing. . . . the countries don't own us. We created them. . . . We're just ourselves. That's what we are in the end. We have to take responsibilities for our actions in the long run, otherwise we deal with the consequences."

References

Apple, M. (1998). *The curriculum: Problems, politics, and possibilities.* Albany: State University of New York Press.
Arendt, H. (1968). *Between past and future.* New York: Penguin Books.
Bauman, Z. (1999). *In Search of Politics.* Cambridge: Polity Press.
Blades, D. (1999). Habilidades básicas para o próximo século: Desenvolvendo a razão, a revolta a responsabilidade dos estudantes (Basic skills for the next century: Developing students' reason, rebellion, and responsibility), in Luiz Heron da Silva (Organizador) Século XXI: qual conhecimento? qual currículo?, pp. 29–38. Petrópolis, RJ, Brasil: Editora Vozes.
Blades, D. (2000) *Curriculum and technology.* Invited paper presentation to the Presidents' Symposium, Canadian Association for Curriculum Studies, Canadian Society for the Study of Education, University of Alberta, May 27.
Boutros-Ghali, B. (1996). Secretary-General says democratization of international relations fundamental requirement for today's world. *UNESCO press release SG/SM/5883.* New York: United Nations Educational, Scientific and Cultural Organization.

Bright, C. (2000) Anticipating environmental "surprise," in L. Starke (Ed.), *State of the World 2000*, pp. 73–85. New York: W. W. Norton.

Brown, L. (2000). Challenges of the New Century, in L. Starke (Ed.), *State of the World 2000*, pp. 12–19. New York: W.W. Norton.

Feinberg, Walter. (1998). *Common schools/uncommon identities: National unity and cultural difference*. New Haven, CN: Yale University Press.

Giddens, A. (2000). *Runaway World: How globalization is reshaping our lives*. London: Routledge.

Kingwell, M. (2000). *The world we want: Virtue, vice and the good citizen*. Toronto: Viking.

Kumano, Y. (1994). *The effects of STS instruction in Japan compared to results reported in the United States*. Tokyo: Azusa Shuppan Sha.

Kymlicka, W. (2001). *Politics in the vernacular: Nationalism, multiculturalism, and citizenship*. London: Oxford University Press.

Leslie, J. (1996). *The end of the world*. London: Routledge.

Levinas, E. (1985). *Ethics and infinity: Conversations with Philippe Nemo*. Richard A. Cohen (Trans.). Pittsburgh: Duquesne University Press.

MacIntyre, A. (1999). *Dependent, rational animals: Why human beings need the virtues*. London: Duckworth.

Mouffe, C. (1993). *The return of the political*. London: Verso.

Nixon, J. (2001). Imagining ourselves into being: Conversing with Hannah Arendt. *Pedagogy, culture and society*, 9, 221–236.

Nussbaum, M. C. (1997). *Cultivating humanity: A classical defense of reform in liberal education*. Cambridge, MA: Harvard University Press.

Orr, D. (1992). *Ecological literacy: Education and the transition to a postmodern world*. Albany: State University of New York Press.

Parker, W., Grossman, D., Kubow, P., Kurth-Schai, R., & Nakayama, S. (1998). Making it work: Implementing multidimensional citizenship, in J. Cogan & R. Derricot (Eds.), *Citizenship for the 21st Century*, pp. 115–137. London: Kogan Page.

Richardson, G. (2004). Global education and the challenge of globalization, in A. Sears & I. Wright (Eds.), *New trends and issues in Canadian Social Studies, 3rd Ed*, pp. 138–149. Vancouver: Pacific Educational Press.

Richardson, G., & Blades, D. (2001). Social studies and science education: Developing world citizenship through interdisciplinary partnerships. *Canadian Social Studies*, 35, 10 pp., retrieved December 9, 2002 from the World Wide Web: http://www.quasar.ualberta.ca/css.

Richardson, G., Blades, D., Kumano, Y., & Karaki, K. (2003). Fostering a global imaginary: The possibilities and paradoxes of Japanese and Canadian students' perceptions of the responsibilities of world citizenship. *Policy Futures in Education*, 1(2), 402–420.

Smith, D. G. (1999). Globalization and Education: prospects for postcolonial pedagogy in a hermeneutic mode. *Interchange*, 30, 1–9.

David Geoffrey Smith

TROUBLES WITH THE SACRED CANOPY: GLOBAL CITIZENSHIP IN A SEASON OF GREAT UNTRUTH

I

When the new *Constitution for Europe* was first drafted, note was made in the Preamble that Europe was a "Christian" civilization. It was quickly recognized with some embarrassment that such a claim might be inappropriate in today's multicultural world, especially given Turkey's overtures to gain admission to the union. The opening sentence of the Preamble was thus recast to read: "Conscious that Europe is a continent that has brought forth civilization . . ." (Constitution Draft, July 2003). While the line's immodesty is transparent to any non-European, what is striking is the how awareness of the immodesty still seems lacking in European "conscious(ness)" itself.

This self-appointment has a long history however, a burden carried under implicitly theological auspices through a God = Christ = Europe equivalencing which extends from 380 CE when Pope Damasus I formed an alliance with Roman emperor Theodosius I. That alliance rehabilitated an earlier temple-state system of the ancient Near East whereby the temple, now controlled by the Christian church, would guarantee the ethical purity of the state, while the state would secure protection of the church in terms of freedom of worship and also the right of its bishops to control doctrine (Mack, 2001). The decree that "There is no salvation outside of the Church" was consolidated at this time, and Europe henceforth assumed its right to define all other peoples in the world as dependent for their salvation on terms Europe defined for them.

Lest these remarks seem extreme and unwarranted, let us recall the words of Europe's preeminent philosopher of the nineteenth century, Georg Wilhelm Friedrich Hegel: " The idea of Christianity has reached its full realization. . . . Europe is absolutely the center and end of universal history. . . . (Europeans) are the carriers of the world spirit, and against that absolute right, the spirit of others people's has no right." (in Dussel, 1995, 20–24). Such ideas became the foundation for Europe's colonization of the entire world in the nineteenth century, and they underwrite the racial profile of global power to this day.

What I would like to do in this paper is examine in more detail the sacred canopy under which social and political theory (including educational theory) in the Western tradition has operated for the last two millennia. This is in light of recent biblical scholarship that has revealed in fairly clear detail how by the fourth century CE the Christian myth had become *historicized* (i.e. turned into a definitive history), and hence how, in a strategy of inversion, a particular parochial history became *mythologized* as a form of universal truth against which all others should be both measured and conditioned. This mythologization of a particular history installed in the world the very definitions of and what it means to be human. The unique problem for today turns on the way that the process of mythologization rendered as taboo any deep critical investigation of the history itself, especially its "underside" (Dussel, 1995, 1996) characterized by mass murder and genocide. This underside is hidden deep within a theology of sacrifice and redemptive suffering, and precisely because it is a theology is it so difficult to question. Yet in the contemporary context the implications of not doing so are profound, dangerous even, and inevitably contributive to unprecedented global instability. What follows here, then, also provides a basis for considering the conditions of citizenship in global times.

One key relation is important to acknowledge right at the beginning. *Europe* also means *America*, in so far as the legacies of America's social and political infrastructure owe more to Europe than to any other set of traditions.* Of course there are differences, some of them profound, having to do with the unique nature of American history since the seventeenth century. Especially relevant is the fact that America is basically Protestant in its Christian predisposition, meaning that for most Americans "The Bible" is the definer of religious truth rather than the culture and tradition of the Catholic Church. The burden of truth therefore is a matter of individual responsibility, personally achieved through a private hermeneutic of scripture. What is important to recognize however is the irony that this privatization mentality now expresses the collective will, such that the American people can become united not only behind patriotic myths that enshrine individual liberty but also behind political and military pogroms against the liberty of those outside of their own regime of truth. Again, this irony has biblical and religious roots that need further investigation. American biblicism has enabled new

---

* *Europe* also means countries like Canada, New Zealand, and Australia that were settled by Europeans in the nineteenth century and whose institutional infrastructures are still defined by the earlier premises of Europe.

forms of political and social theory organized around tropes of apocalypticism and eschatology, which are what makes current times increasingly ominous at the level of everyday awareness. Apocalypticism and eschatology also provide the justification for new forms of military aggression in American foreign policy, and special self-granted license to engage in acts that in any other context would be considered criminal. One of the central tasks of scholarship today, therefore, must be to dehistoricize the Western myth of divine appointment, so that the Euro-American nexus can simply assume its place among equals at the table of globalization's deliberations. This is particularly a requirement of Jews and Christians, whose shared tradition of divine chosenness, while pivotal for their respective self-identities, is also deeply problematic historically speaking, i.e. many of the claims about, say, right of land ownership, cannot be verified through concrete historical research (Cantor, 1995; Harpur, 2004), only declared as pronouncements of belief.

Much of what has been said above is not new. What may be new, or at least crystallized in starker terms than previously, is that Europe's sole remaining child superpower, the United States (the Soviet Union was the other child superpower of Europe), has embarked on a program of preemptive warfare against all those peoples, nations, and cultures of the world who refuse to ally themselves in favor of what America desires. This is now carried out behind a rhetorical mask bespeaking the virtues of peace, freedom, and democracy, and a demonization of all naysayers as betrayers of universal truth. The consequence is an inversion of language such that for American foreign policy, peace-seeking means warmongering, freedom means enslavement to puerile notions of greed and undisciplined power, democracy means unfettered electoral fraud and manipulation in the service of predetermined outcomes, and evil is embodied most especially by those who declaim it as the special character of Others. Under such conditions, what is a teacher supposed to tell her students about citizenship in today's world? In a season of great untruth, is there a theory of human nature that can survive such butchering of relations between word and deed? If there is, surely every child has a right to be nurtured by it, for the sake of a more hopeful future.

In case there remains today anyone who actually believes that the political and military maneuvering behind American domestic and foreign policy have humanity's best interests at heart, it is important to reiterate in the clearest terms possible the basic objectives of the Grand Game in play (Brzezinski, 1997, Chossudovsky, 2002). There is only one interest at work really, which is the complete domination of contemporary global order, the chief means to which at the moment is a securing of gas and oil resources around the world as the absolute, non-negotiable condition upon which the future of America, at least as it knows itself to be in the present, depends (see Yergin, 1992). All other public pronouncements and rhetorical embellishments about freedom and democracy are simply a mask of this basic truth. The right to rule is taken as a divine right, secularized through logics of individual liberty and the right to private property. In the meantime, war in the Middle East is designed to secure the huge resources there. The invasion of Afghanistan is a pretext for securing a pipeline from the Caucasus through to the Arabian Sea. Financing the Chechin rebels is a way to keep Russia from securing the huge resources of the Baku region of the Caspian Sea: ditto for financing the election of Yushchenko in the Ukraine. Establishing military bases throughout Central Asia, along with sending in evangelical Christian missionaries, is the strategy for keeping China out of the region. Befriending Pakistan is the way to contain India. Issuing warnings to North Korea is, among other things, a pretext for keeping military bases in South Korea. Organizing street opposition among the middle classes to democratically elected Hugo Chavez in Venezuela is an attempt to secure the huge Maracaibo reserves. Similar efforts routinely take place in West Africa—Liberia, Ivory Coast, Nigeria, etc.—and many other parts of the world, such as the Philippines.

Nor is the U.S. terrorism at work in all of these projects reserved for Other peoples alone. One day, the truth of 9/11 may finally be made more transparently public.* Currently the structures of psychological denial are too firmly in place, and the truth is too horrendous to contemplate for most people still clinging to a fantasy of political integrity. The facts are that, like Roosevelt at the time of Pearl Harbor, the Bush administration knew months, even years in advance of 9/11 that an attack was imminent. The strategy became to 'play along', even paving the way with ease of passport use, enabling the use of flight schools, and demanding a "stand down" of military defense aircraft on the fateful morning—all for the purpose of ensuring the success of the mission. The Trade Center towers had already been wired for a controlled detonation, so that during the collapse there would be minimal collateral damage. As with Pearl Harbor, a powerful symbolic act of destruction from an enemy was needed to legitimize and mobilize support for what had already been long planned, which were the invasions of Afghanistan and Iraq. Osama bin Laden and Saddam Hussein were/are simply semiotic necessities.

Most disturbing perhaps is the mendacity surrounding the language and practice of democracy. The support of dictatorships around the world which serve corporate American interests has been recognized for over a hundred years. In the present context, the Bush administration has corrupted the processes of democracy within America itself, not only to win its election in 2000 (Moore, 2002), but also in 2004. According to a notarized affidavit signed by computer programmer Clint Curtis, he was solicited by Florida Republican Representative Tom Feeney to write a customized Windows-based program to suppress Democratic votes on touch-screen voting machines. Curtis complied and delivered the program to Feeney. The program was designed to be "undetectable" and fully capable of "delivering the vote to George" (Madsen, 2004). Ray C. Lemme, a senior investigator with the Florida Department of Transport Inspector General's Office traced out the intricate connections between Feeney and the Florida governor's office of

---

*For background reading related to what immediately follows regarding 9/11, see Ahmed (2002), Chossudovsky (2002), Griffin (2004, 2005), and numerous web links at Online journal.com.

Jeb Bush. Lemme then provided details to the *Daytona Beach News Journal* of how Jeb Bush himself attempted to halt his investigation. On Sunday, June 29th, 2003, Lemme was found dead in a Georgia motel room.

Elsewhere (Smith, 2003) I have outlined the contents of a document released in 2002 titled "National Security Strategy for the United States of America" (NSSUSA), which detailed American global strategy for the Bush administration. The report begins with an announcement that the twentieth century has brought forth a "*single* sustainable model for national success: freedom, democracy and free enterprise," a model to be protected "across the globe and across the ages." Particularly striking are recommendations regarding weapons by means of which the new imperial war can be waged. NSSUSA insists, "we must make use of every tool in our arsenal." What do these include? Weapons of mass destruction are on the list, particularly "low-yield" nuclear weapons and the use of depleted uranium. Biological weapons programs have been updated "to produce systems that will degrade the war fighting capabilities of potential adversaries." The generic language deliberately leaves open the possibility of bioterrorist attacks on civilian populations to disable national economies, *qua* SARS, Mad Cow, and Hoof and Mouth disease.

Of particular concern today, not mentioned in the NSSUSA report, are weapons capable of mass destruction under the banner of nature, or natural disaster. This banner provides perfect cover from any public exposure of the destruction's origins. The HAARP weapon, funded largely by big oil companies such as Vice President Cheney's Halliburton Corporation, is capable of controlling environmental conditions on the earth, as well as causing earthquakes anywhere in the world. (Solomatin, 2004; Chossudovsky, 2004). HAARP is the acronym for High-frequency Active Auroral Research Program. High-frequency transmitter facilities can heat the earth environment up to the state of plasma by means of pumping ions into the atmosphere, then redirecting them to specific targets back on earth. As described by Yuru Solomatin, Deputy Secretary of the Ukranian Committee for Economic Policy, Nature Management and for the Liquidation of Chernobyl Consequences, "the owners of this weapon are able to program floods, twisters and storms, even earthquakes in any region of the planet. It is also possible to paralyse civil and military surveillance systems, and even to affect the mentality of whole nations."

According to Greg Mallo (2005) the U.S. is now also fielding a new tactical and strategic nuclear military capability described as an "earth-penetrating" nuclear device. Deployed and developed in secret, without public or congressional debate, the blast energy of the weapon is capable of producing huge shock waves in the earth's deep crust that can destabilize the fault lines of the tectonic plates on which visible earth structures and the nations and peoples of the world reside. Interestingly enough, the three largest earthquakes of the last several years have been in Islamic countries (Iran, Indonesia) that control huge petroleum deposits, or like Turkey, control key venues of petroleum transportation.

These efforts are being conducted under a deliberate campaign of "information warfare" involving the deliberate spread of falsehoods as a weapon of war. As reported by the Research Unit for Political Economy (RUPE, 2003, 77) of Delhi,

India, a secret army has been established to unite the CIA, covert military action, and specialists in information deception.

II

What I would like to do in this section of the paper is discuss how such a malignant state of affairs could possibly have come into being and how it could be enacted by its players with such an air of innocence and seeming lack of guilt. I have already alluded briefly to the theological infrastructure that scaffolds the particular form of consciousness whereby mass murder and deception can be conducted in the name of Truth. But this needs further elaboration, and here I wish to draw on the work of two sources: a) Argentine philosopher, now living in exile in Mexico, Enrique Dussel; and b) Theological literature on the role of sacrifice in the creation of culture, especially the work of Uta Ranke-Heinemann (1994), (Burton Mack, 2001), and Walter Burkert, Rene Girard and Jonathan Z. Smith (in Hamerton-Kelly, 1987).

The ascendance of America to the role of solo global superpower represents the final point in the long trajectory of European modernity that began with the Columban landfall in the Caribbean in 1492. This was the moment when the center of global power began to shift to Europe (henceforth now "West" relative to "East") from the Middle East and Central Asia which had been under control of the Muslim caliphates for the previous eight hundred years and which had controlled the wealth feeding Europe through the silk and spice routes. The system of global power that evolved sequent to Columbus has been named by numerous scholars (Amin, Wallerstein, etc.) as "The 1492 World System," and basically it has lasted until the present time, although as America self-destructs, the global patterns are shifting (see Amin 2001), but such is the topic for a later discussion.

As Dussel describes it, the 1492 World System is underwritten by a two-fold logic. On the surface, the logic is that of "emancipative reason," which found its clearest articulation in the philosophy of Immanuel Kant in the eighteenth century. To be human, said Kant, is to choose freedom. To refuse to choose freedom is to remain in "perpetual immaturity." Dussel begins his philosophical explorations with the Spanish conquests of "Latin" America, when the Catholic Church legitimized the slaughter of Aztec, Inca, and Maya civilizations on the basis of their refusal of Christian freedom,* but this dream of freedom is a central motif within the most ancient Jewish and Christian visions, from the Abramic myth of leaving the constraints of home and family for the land of promise through the Mosaic exodus of emancipation from Egypt to the land of milk and honey, to the earliest Christian call to live under the immediate Reign of God and the "glorious freedom of the gospel" (Romans 8:21).

---

*For a detailed discussion of the theological debate within the Roman Catholic church in the sixteenth century surrounding the decision to legitimize genocide, see Dussel 1995. I have summarized the contents of this debate in Smith 2005.

If freedom is the surface myth of Christo-European modernity, it is Dussel's contribution to identify its underside, which is the myth of sacrifice, operating as a silenced, not-to-be-spoken-in-public shadow of the myth of emancipative reason. Again, Dussel takes the sacrifice of Amerindian populations as paradigmatic, but the same dynamic is already apparent in the earliest Judeo-Christian mythic accounts. Entering the Promised Land under the military leadership of Joshua (Joshua 1–24) requires the crushing of an enemy and a massive land grab in the name of divine intention. The sacrifice of the Other is simply a necessity in service of a greater self-defined truth. Under Jeshua (Jesus), Christians take up residence in the new kingdom of God, leaving (sacrificing) family and friends for membership in the new, divinely appointed family, forever defining themselves against the kingdoms of this world (John 18:36). In the Abramic myth, the willingness to sacrifice even one's own children (the story of Isaac) is taken as a test of faith in the promise of the freedom of God. This theme of infanticide is taken to the fullest extreme in the Christian myth. As a sign of his love for the world, God sacrifices his only son, with the promise that whoever believes in the son, so sacrificed, and therefore by implication whoever also is willing to sacrifice themselves in such a way, or their children, will have found the way to live forever (John 3:16).

German psychotherapist Tilman Moser (in Ranke-Heinemann, 1994, 281) has written of how the logic of sacrifice installs in the Western imaginary a neurotic crisis that is incapable of being healed from within itself. If the logic is, basically, "because I love you I have to kill you," or "if you really love me then you will understand/accept my killing of you," then certain other dynamics also come into play. On a personal level, I am reduced to self-hatred when I find myself unwilling to pay the price of full self-sacrifice or am unwilling to accept your love if it requires my death. This results in an aggressive inversion whereby self-hatred gets turned back on the perpetrator, and the Other becomes the object of my own terror, which I must destroy if I am to survive. On a collective and political level, the lessons are obvious.

Contemporary American domestic and foreign policy issues from this deep neurosis. At home, the poor, the homeless, the disenfranchised, and the young are filled with self-loathing because what is offered in solution to their difficulties is so impossible. Hence they await sacrifice in the name of God or Truth whose contemporary secular name is The Market (Loy, 2002). If those ripe for sacrifice could only choose their freedom, they could live forever. Their failure to choose (think Choice Theory in education) is itself a choice—of consequences that may be regrettable in some sentimental sense, but not to be regretted in the larger scheme of things. Indeed, sacrifice of the nonchoosers of freedom is taken as a moral necessity for the future of the species. In terms of foreign policy, George W. Bush was perfectly clear in his second inaugural speech: "If you desire freedom, America will help you. If you don't, America will destroy you" (paraphrase). Such is the condition of our time. The sacred canopy has broken open to reveal its insanity.

III

Any discussion about global citizenship today must come to terms with the kind of conditions I have laid out above. These conditions have to do with one nation-state being determined to control the terms of citizenship itself. The conditions are inhabited by logics and rituals of the sacred that place a taboo over deep critical analysis and are underwritten by a mythical structure that ensures into perpetuity the second-class status of all Others within a global community. Even in terms of economic development, peoples that do show obeisance to The Market find themselves working against a paradigm within which they have no hope of parity (Chang, 2002). This is because the laws and enactments of The Market are predetermined according to the logics and rituals of the sacred that have just been outlined: play the game our way, but then if you are too successful, well we have the right to secure ourselves. Or: We love you, therefore become like us, but then we may have to kill you.

In this section of the chapter, I would like to consider what citizenship education might look like given the global conditions as outlined. I take this up as a curricular question, but it has its pedagogical aspect in the sense that pedagogy involves introducing students to 'the story of life,' a narrative work. From the perspective of this chapter, the central narrative of European "Christian" civilization needs a basic revisitation particularly from the perspective of those living outside of its power base.

One proposal is that discussions about citizenship and citizenship education today must be cast through what can be termed a *Comparative Discourse of Empire* (CDE). To learn to see Europe/America as only one empire, and only the latest, within the world's long experience with many, has a number of important virtues. For one thing, it becomes possible to understand the empire as an "episode" (Amin, 2001) within the human story, not a final triumph announcing the "end of history" (Fukuyama, 1992). This in turn allows a more self-conscious fracturing of the sacred canopy so that the underlying assumptions of the empire can be jarred loose for a more profound critical investigation than has hitherto been possible.

This is not to say that the West does not have a "critical" tradition (*qua* Kant); indeed possessing it is a point of hubris. But that is also the point; the hubris is blind to its nemesis. As Enrique Dussel has argued so strenuously, the paradigmatics of Western consciousness are completely self-enclosed, blind and deaf to all voices outside of their own logics and self-understandings. Again, this is because of the self-definition of divine appointment. So understanding the empire as an episode within a Comparative Discourse of Empire grants a new kind of status to the empire's nemesis. The nemesis becomes the Voice from the Outside, refusing the Empire's universal authority and demanding a new kind of partnership within a newly emerging global community. Dussel addresses this as attending to "the underside of modernity." It can also be spoken of in terms of listening to those "outside of History," taking the modern notion of History as inexorably Eurocentric in its basic formulation.

A key aspect of attending to the underside of modernity requires that the undiluted suffering of those making the 'freedom' of Europe/America possible has to be brought into the center of deliberations regarding human futures. Furthermore, this suffering has to be brought to consciousness in stark and vivid terms. The slaughter of five hundred thousand Iraqi children since 1990 (McMurtry, 1998) due to aerial bombardment and devastation of social infrastructures (water, sanitation, health care, etc.) somehow has to register deeply within the dream structure of Washington policy wonks and war gamers. The screams, the pleadings, the endless crying, the vacant stares of trauma, the open, bleeding, pus-filled wounds, the limbless corpses, the orphaned masses, the napalmed faces: Mr. Bush, Mr. Rumsfeld, Mr. Wolfowitz, please take a seat. Witness these things, smell them, think of your own children, then think of a better justification than Madeleine Albright provided when queried on the matter: "We think the price was worth it" (McMurtry, 2002, 68). Rest assured, humanity will not stand for this kind of delusion much longer. If this is your god, we want no more of 'him.'

Iraq of course is only the latest in a long line of Others whose suffering has been silenced in the name of Freedom. Also to be heard from are the ghosts of Latin America of the last five hundred years (Galeano, 1997). Let us hear from those whose lives purchased Europe's 'theory' of liberty: from the Aztecs whose blood flowed ankle deep down the streets of Tenochtitlan while Cortez watched with a priest by his side; from the tin miners still coughing blood in their Bolivian graves; and from African slaves whipped into submission by their luxuriating plantation owners. Let us hear the real story from the Hutus and the Tutsis of Central Africa, of where they got their guns and machetes and why. And let us hear why it is so important for American and European companies to sustain such perpetual massacres for the sake of titanium, bauxite, diamonds, tungsten, molybdenum, and oil. Then let us decide if these things are really what is needed to live decent human lives. Let us hear from the ghosts of Geronimo, and the Blackfoot Confederacy, and Batoche, not because the horrors of the past can ever be fully redressed, but because unless the ghosts are heard from the horrors will go on being repeated.

A Comparative Discourse of Empire, then, allows the possibility of seeing through the delusion whereby a particular logic of freedom is purchased through a particular logic of sacrifice and under which murder and genocide carried on in the name of those logics cannot be named as such. Murder and genocide is what Other people engage in: Judeo-Christian acts of murder and genocide are inexorably self-defined as necessary acts of redemption.

There is a related matter as well: It is precisely because a particular logic of freedom is purchased through a particular logic of sacrifice that the *nature* of the particular freedom in question cannot be interrogated, because those who could do so are silenced or dead. Without understanding the sources and origins of their particular freedom, those who possess it are henceforth conditioned to be deluded about its essential qualities. Indeed the very rhetoric of democracy and free elections is now used as an instrument of Empire itself. Democracy no longer requires real terms; it can be fully manufactured and manipulated at the whim of the new Caesars as a requirement of the predetermined order.

Within the logic of the current Empire, the freedom/sacrifice linkage is also what allows an amnesia regarding the historically constructed religion/Market conflation, and then in turn the role that The Market plays in the construction of the logics of freedom. As Dussel has clearly outlined (1996), it was the extraordinary wealth that flowed into Europe sequent to the Spanish conquest of Latin America that afforded the luxury of the personal logics of liberty. "Freedom" as a defining trope of European modernity cannot be traced to intellectual or religious traditions primarily; instead, its very source is money. In America, by the writers of the Constitution, freedom (and democracy) were never originally conceived as being for all, only for property owners, who themselves were the new bourgeoisie from the new mercantile classes of seventeenth century Europe. Hence today, a critique of the logics of freedom determining the shape of global order must inevitably involve a critique of the circulating logic of money (McMurtry, 2001, 2002), a link well understood by the attackers of the World Trade Center, the quintessential symbol of American wealth/empire.

This analysis brings to the fore a realization that more than anything, what is needed in the world today is a new logic of freedom. The imperial logic has finally exposed itself as a death-trap except for the increasingly few who can afford its purchase through the sacrifice of Others. At home, one of the conditions of that sacrifice is an ensuring that people remain enslaved to the very logic of freedom that is killing them. Media control is a preeminent imperial requirement. For educators this raises the question of where sources may be found for a new kind of public knowledge that can genuinely provide insight into the operations of the imperial order, so that a new curricular narrative may be woven that is more inclusive and just and free of the neurotic circuits that currently inhabit public education by virtue of its conditioning within the freedom/sacrifice nexus.* Pedagogically it means we must learn to love our children simply for themselves and be willing to give up the fantasy that by killing them we will make the gods happy and hence secure our future.

A primary requirement for a new logic of freedom is to break the particular connection between freedom and sacrifice that the current imperial logic espouses. At the moment, my freedom requires your death, and if to be free means to be free like me, then ultimately there will be only one person remaining at the end of Armageddon. No, an understanding of freedom appropriate to global times requires not your death but mine, that is, the death of a particular concept of identity, whereby identity is assumed to be secured only through the abolition of its alterity. Putting it in Christian language, and to bring the matter back to the original problematic of Christocentric Europeanism, what is required involves "loving

---

*Most 'alternative' information today is found on the Internet, as web sites such as Onlinejournal.com, Black Radical Congress, Center for Globalization Research, and the World Social Forum, etc. I also draw attention to the Public Knowledge Project, organized by John Willinsky at the University of British Columbia, Canada.

your enemies." Fully understood, this is not a uniquely Christian injunction. The psychological dynamics are very well understood in Buddhism and other Asian wisdom traditions such as Taoism. As well, it is central in Jungian psychoanalysis of the "shadow" in human experience (Zweig and Abram 1991). Basically it is not so much a moral injunction as a recognition that who or what I think is my enemy is actually a deep and inseparable part of myself. In Hinduism, this is expressed in the Sanskrit words *tuam asi sat*—that you are, or you are that. Identity is not to be understood dualistically, even as an I-Thou proposition such as that of Buber or Levinas. Instead, there is an acceptance that whenever I think of myself, I at the same time think of you, because you are part of me and vice versa. To love my enemies is to love myself in a more full way; it is also to refuse the paranoia that inevitably arises through a dualistic understanding of identity. What I think I hate is actually what I need to understand myself in a more fully human way. Clinging to my hatred marks a refusal to grow up.

Buddhist social theorist David Loy (2003) has written eloquently of "loving the world as one's own body," which draws attention to the ecological and political implications of a nondualistic theory of persons. In terms of contemporary global realities, as America self-destructs as a global power because of its imperial venturing, citizenship education can begin formulating notions of human community based on the profound interdependence of human requirements and of human-earth relations. Already, there are signs of this in the new *Constitution for Europe*, with its emphasis on "unity in diversity." Pedagogically, one can think of education no longer in terms of training for the requirements of The Market, but more in terms of realizing the gifts of the young, so that together we may venture more creatively into the future.

Within the comparative discourse of empire, two features typically mark an empire in decline, what Paul Kennedy (1989) names as "imperial overstretch" and Walden Bello (2002) "a loss of the moral right to rule." Today it is appropriate to ponder these words relative to our shared global circumstances.

References

Ahmed, N. (2002). *The war on freedom: How and why America was attacked on September 11, 2001*. Joshua Tree, CA: Tree of Life Publications.
Amin, S. (2001). *Obsolescent capitalism*. New York: Monthly Review Press.
Bello, W. (2002). *Deglobalization: Ideas for a new world economy*. London: Zed Books.
Brzezinski, Z. (1997). *The grand chessboard: American primacy and its geostrategic imperatives*. New York: Basic Books.
Cantor, N. (1995). *The sacred chain: A history of the Jews*. New York: HarperPerennial.
Chang, H. (2002). *Kicking away the ladder: Developmental strategy in historical perspective*. London: Anthem Press.
Chossudovsky, M. (2001). Washington's New World Order weapons have the ability to trigger climate change. www.globalresearch.ca/articles/CHO201A.p.html.
Chossudovsky, M. (2002). *War and globalization*. Toronto: James Lorimer Publications.

Constitution of Europe Draft. (2003). Preamble. www.europa.eu.int/futurum/constitution/index_en.htm.
Dussel, E. (1995). *The invention of the Americas: Eclipse of 'the other' and the myth of modernity*. (Trans. M. Barber). New York: Continuum.
Dussel, E. (1996). *The underside of modernity: Apel, Rorty, Taylor and the philosophy of liberation*. (Trans. and Ed. E. Mendieta). Atlantic Highlands, NJ: Humanities Press.
Fukuyama, F. (1993). *The end of history and the last man*. New York: Avon Press.
Galeano, E. (1997). *Open veins of Latin America: Five centuries of the pillage of a continent*. New York: Monthly Review Press.
Griffin, D. (2004). *The new Pearl Harbor*. San Francisco: Olive Branch Press.
Griffin, D. (2005). *The 9/11 Commission: Omissions and distortions*. San Francisco: Olive Branch Press.
Hamerton-Kelly, R. (1987) (Ed.). *Violent origins: Ritual killing and cultural formation*. Stanford, CA: Stanford University Press.
Harpur, T. (2004). *The pagan Christ: Recovering the lost light*. Toronto: Thomas Allen Publishers.
Kennedy, P. (1989). *The rise and fall of the great powers*. New York: Vintage Books.
Loy, D. (2002). The market as god. In *A Buddhist history of the West* (pp. 56–70). New York: State University of New York Press.
Loy, D. (2003). Loving the world as our own body. In *The great awakening: Buddhist social theory* (pp. 171–194). Boston: Wisdom Books.
Mack, B. (2001). *The Christian myth: Origins, logic and legacy*. New York: Continuum.
Madsen, W. (2004). Texas to Florida: White House-linked clandestine operation paid for "vote switching" software. *www.onlinejournal.com* December 6th.
Mallo, G. (2005). Burrowing nuclear bomb: Summary on The Sub-Criticals. www.prop1.org/2000/subcrit/97newuk.htm.
McMurtry, J. (1998). *Unequal freedoms: The global market as an ethical system*. Toronto: Garamond Press.
McMurtry, J. (2002). *Value wars: The global market versus the life economy*. London: Pluto Press.
Moore, M. (2001). A very American coup. In *Stupid white men* (pp. 1–28). New York: Regan Books.
Ranke-Heinemann, U. (1994). *Putting away childish things*. San Francisco: HarperSanFrancisco.
Research Unit for Political Economy. (2003). *Behind the invasion of Iraq*. New York: Monthly Review Press.
Smith, D. (2003). On enfrauding the public sphere, the futility of empire and the future of knowledge after 'America.' *Policy Futures in Education 1(3)*, 488–503.
Smith, D. (2005). Not rocket science: On the limits of conservative pedagogy. In K. Cooper and R. White (Eds.), *The practical critical educator* (pp. 51–64). Dordrecht, NL: Kluwer.
Solomatin, Y. (2004). HAARP poses global threat. www.bariumblues.com/haarp_geophysical_ weapon.htm.
Wallerstein, I. (Ed.). (1997). *Geopolitics and Geoculture: Essays on the changing world system*. London: Cambridge University Press.
Yergin, D. (1992). *The prize: The epic quest for oil, money and power*. New York: Simon and Schuster.
Zweig, C., & Abram, J. (1991). *Meeting the shadow: The hidden power of the dark side of human nature*. New York: Jeremy P. Tarcher.

CONTRIBUTORS

David Blades is currently the Associate Dean, Teacher Education and Director of the Centre for Excellence in Teaching and Understanding Science at the University of Victoria in Victoria, British Columbia, Canada. He is a principal researcher in the CRYSTALs project, an initiative to promote excellence in Canadian school science. He studies the implications of post-structural thought to curriculum change, particularly in the areas of science education, multiculturalism and citizenship education. Among his publications is *Procedures of Power and Curriculum Change: Foucault and the Quest for Possibilities in Science* Education (Peter Lang, 1998). When he has the chance he and his family can be found sailing the Pacific Northwest.

Terry Carson is Professor in the Department of Secondary Education at the University of Alberta. His research and teaching interests include teacher identity, curriculum studies, and multicultural/anti-racist education. His recent work focuses on teacher identity and socially transformative change; and on the challenges of accomplishing citizenship education in pluralistic democratic societies through the public school.

Kent den Heyer is an assistant professor at Kent State University. He has taught a range of subjects and grades in schools and has developed workshops on citizenship and democratic education for international scholars. Dr. den Heyer has published and presented research internationally on student and teacher interpretations of the ways that social change occurs, psychoanalytic approaches to anti-racist education, and curriculum theory.

A professor at the University of Calgary, **Yvonne Hébert** specializes in cultural, political, and social issues in education. Her books include the two volume set, *Indian Education in Canada* (UBC Press, 1986 and 1987); *L'évolution de l'école francophone en milieu minoritaire* (CMLR, 1993), *Citizenship in Transformation in Canada* (UT Press, 2002), and *Negotiating Transcultural Lives: Belongings and Social Capital among Youth in Comparative Perspective* (V&R Unipress, Germany, 2005).

Dr. Emery J. Hyslop-Margison is an Assistant Professor in the Department of Education at Concordia University in Montreal. He recently received a Tier II Canada Research Chair nomination for his research in career education and democratic learning.

Ingrid Johnston is Associate Professor in the Department of Secondary Education and Associate Dean of Research and Graduate Studies in the Faculty of Education at the University of Alberta. Her research and teaching interests focus on postcolonial literary theories and pedagogies, English education, adolescent literature and questions of cultural difference and teacher education. Her book *Re-mapping Literary Worlds: Postcolonial Pedagogy in Practice* (Peter Lang, 2003) will appear in Chinese translation with Education Science Publishing House in Beijing in 2006.

Lisa W. Loutzenheiser is an Assistant Professor of Curriculum Studies at the University of British Columbia. Her research interests include marginalized youth, gender and sexuality studies and anti-oppressive education at secondary and graduate levels.

Lori B. MacIntosh is a PhD candidate at the University of British Columbia. Her research and writing focus on issues of sexuality and gender construed as complex systems of culturally organized practices. Lori is currently a research associate on a three-year project looking at queer women, cultural politics of representation, and engagements with media.

Jyoti Mangat is a Doctoral Candidate at the University of Alberta where she is doing interdisciplinary work with the departments of English and Secondary Education. Her research interests include postcolonialism, curriculum theory, literature and questions of identity construction.

William F. Pinar teaches curriculum theory at the University of British Columbia, where he holds a Canada Research Chair and directs the Centre for the Study of the Internationalization of Curriculum Studies. Pinar is the author of *Race, Re-*

ligion and a Curriculum of Reparation (Palgrave Macmillan, 2006), *The Synoptic Text Today and other essays: Curriculum Development after the Reconceptualization* (Peter Lang, 2006), *What Is Curriculum Theory?* (Lawrence Erlbaum, 2004), *Autobiography, Politics, and Sexuality* (Peter Lang, 1994), and *The Gender of Racial Politics and Violence in America* (Peter Lang, 2001).

George H. Richardson is an associate professor in the Department of Secondary Education at the University of Alberta and Coordinator of International Initiatives for the Faculty of Education. His research interests include the role of education in national identity formation, citizenship education, multicultural and international education and action research. Among his publications, he is the author of *The Death of the Good Canadian: Teachers National Identities and the Social Studies Curriculum* (Peter Lang, 2002). He is editor of the journal, *Canadian Social Studies*.

Alan Sears is a Professor of Social Studies Education at the University of New Brunswick in Canada. He has been a social studies teacher for more than 25 years working at all levels from primary to graduate school. In addition to co-editing *Trends and Issues in Canadian Social Studies* (Pacific Educational Press, 1997) and *Challenges and Prospects for Canadian Social Studies* (Pacific Educational Press, 2004). He has published extensively in the area of citizenship education. He is Chief Regional Editor for Canada for the International Journal of Citizenship and Teacher Education.

David Geoffrey Smith is a Professor of Education in the Department of Secondary Education at the University of Alberta. He teaches and researches in the areas of Globalization Studies, Curriculum Theory and Asian Wisdom traditions. His major papers have been collected in *Pedagon: Interdisciplinary Essays in the Human Sciences, Pedagogy and Culture* (Peter Lang, 1999), *Globalization and Postmodern Pedagogy* (Beijing Educational Sciences Press 2001), and *Trying to Teach in a Season of Great Untruth* (Sense Publications, forthcoming).

Hans Smits is an Associate Professor, and Associate Dean in the Division of Teacher Preparation, Faculty of Education, University of Calgary. He has worked at the university level for about ten years, and prior to that was a junior and senior high social studies teacher. He has written in the areas of social studies education, action research and hermeneutics, and currently is focusing primarily on research into teacher education.

Jennifer Tupper is a former high school social studies teacher and is currently an assistant professor in the Faculty of Education at the University of Regina. Her research interests include citizenship and social studies, teacher education, and teaching for social (in)justice. Most importantly, she is mother to three-and-a-half year old Ayla.

Lori Wilkinson is an Assistant Professor in the Department of Sociology at the University of Manitoba. In 2004, she was awarded a Visiting Research Fellowship at the Refugee Studies Centre, University of Oxford. Currently, she is Secretary Treasurer of the Canadian Ethnic Studies Association and sits on several other academic committees and research panels. She is actively involved in research on the life course transitions of immigrant and refugee youth and on the health and well-being of immigrant children.

INDEX

agency
  in the classroom, 101
  historical, 91–2
  and idealization, 87
  individual, 90
  and learning, 61
  and social change, 89, 92–3
  student views, 86
agora, 6, 120, 121, 122
ahimsa, 3, 29
Air India disaster. *See* "The Management of Grief" (Mukherjee)
alienation of citizens, 16, 17, 18–9, 26–7
Americans, 20, 26
Arendt, Hannah, 57, 58–9, 116, 117
Arnold, Matthew, 78
Association of Southern Women for the Prevention of Lynching, 109
Atonement (McEwan), 60
Auden, W. H., 58
Australia, civic education policies, 15, 16
  See also Civic Experts Group

Bannerji, Himani, 74
Bauman, Zygmund, 121

Bellah, Robert, 58
Bennett, Jane, 56, 64
Bliss, Michael, 16, 18
Bloom, Harold, 79
Borgmann, Albert, 28
Brand, David, 21
British Advisory Group on Citizenship, 16
British colonialism, 77
Brown v. Board of Education, 89
Buddhism, 134
Bush administration (George W.), 126–7, 128, 130
Bush, Jeb, 127–8
Butler, Judith, 55

Callan, Eamonn, 57
Canada
  civic education policies, 15
  cultural diversity, 31, 32, 34, 67–74
  racism in, 70–1
  suburban diversity, 69
Canadian Charter of Rights and Freedoms (1982), 34
Carson, Terry, 3
Centre for Canadian Studies, 16

Centre for Citizenship Education (Hong Kong Institute of Education), 15
Centre for Research on Information About Canada, 15
Christianity
    European and Western history, 124
    freedom myth, 129–30
    love of the Other/enemy, 133–4
    mythologization, 125
    sacrifice myth, 130
    theology, 6
citizenship
    and diversity, 46, 48–9
    global, 2, 5–6, 115–7, 118
    and Greek rationalism, 46–7
    vs. historical agency, 92
    history vs. memory, 60
    idea vs. practice, 57
    liberal vs. conservative views, 86, 118
    and national identity, 57, 95
    and oppression, 52–3
    participatory, 48
    as a practice of learning, 63, 120
    and privilege, 48
    and the self, 51, 56, 100
    temporal aspects, 57
    universality, 46
citizenship domains, 5, 33–4, 36–7, 37 fig. 2
Citizenship on Trial: Interdisciplinary Perspectives on the Political Socialization of Adolescents (McGill University), 21
civic education
    cult mentality, 21–2
    as game playing, 50–1
    and global citizenship, 117
    and the humanities, 3
    modern history of, 14–5
    and religious cults, 3
    and schools, 3, 21
    and social studies, 26, 49–52
    See also curricula, and citizenship education
Civic Experts Group (Australia), 15, 16
Clark, Frank, 108
Collins, Winfield, 109
Commission on Interracial Cooperation, 109
Comparative Discourse of Empire, 131, 132
Conduct, and decision-making, 59
conservative ideology, and citizenship, 47–8
Constitution for Europe, 124, 134
Council of Europe, 15

Council of Ministers of Education Pan-Educational Research Agenda (Canada), 15, 20
Crimson Tide (film), 21
The Cult of Efficiency (Stein), 14
curricula
    and citizenship education, 26
    fragmentation of, 26, 27, 28
    and ideology, 13–4
    See also social studies, curricula
Curtis, Clint, 127

democracy
    evolutionary nature of, 1, 48
    false universalism, 45–7, 48
    knowledge of vs. belief in, 17
    and the public space, 27–8
    and sacrifice, 132
democratic dispositions, 33
democratic values, 19–20, 35 fig. 1, 36, 39
den Heyer, Kent, 5
Dewey, John, 27, 62
disenchantment, 62
Doctorow, E. L., 27
Dominion Institute, 16, 18
The Dream of Scipio (Pears), 58, 59
Dussel, Enrique, 129, 130, 131, 133
Dyer (anti-lynching) legislation, 108
Dyer, Gwynne, 20

Edible Ballot Society, 25
educational reform, 13, 14
election fraud, 127–8
Elections Canada, 16
Eliasoph, Nina, 52
Eliot, T. S., 78
Emancipation Proclamation, 107
The Enchantment of Modern Life (Bennett), 56
English Advisory Group on Citizenship, 15
English (language arts), 77, 78–9, 80, 81
Equite Club, 106
"Escape from Politics" (Univ. of Alberta Symposium), 25, 28
ethics, and the self, 64–5
Europeans, and racism, 20
Europe, civic education policies, 15

Fairclough, Ellen, 14
Feeney, Tom, 127
feminism, 4

freedom of speech, 17
fundamentalism, 30

Gadamer, H. G., 55
Gandhi, Mohandas K., 29–30
gays and lesbians, 98
  See also queer theory
"George Blair," 88–9
Giddens, Anthony, 121
globalization
  and *agora*, 120–1
  and alienation of youth, 25
  and cultural values, 38
  and democratic values, 31
  and global citizenship, 2, 5–6, 117
Granatstein, Jack, 16, 18
Grant, S. G., 88–9
Greene, Maxine, 28, 80–1

HAARP (High-Frequency Active Auroral Research Program), 128
Hackman, Gene, 21
Hahn, Carole, 16, 17, 18–9, 20
Harris, Barbara, 106
Hastings College of Law, 106
Hébert, Yvonne, 3
Hegel, Georg Wilhelm Friedrich, 124
historical amnesia, 58
history
  curriculum, 88
  as embodied experience, 60–1
  and European/American empire, 131, 133, 134
  and idealizations of citizenship, 85–6
  as narration of memory, 60, 64–5, 90
  study and knowledge of, 16, 17, 18, 26
  teaching and teachers, 86, 88
Hollis, James, 30
Hong Kong, civic education policies, 15
Hong Kong Institute of Education, 15
human dignity, 37
  See also citizenship domains
Hyslop-Margison, Emery, 3

identity
  and the capable learner, 61
  and citizenship, 4
  and dualism, 134
  and historical agency, 92–3
  and history, 85–6

identity *(continued)*
  and the imagination, 93
  and literature, 80
  national, 14, 57, 81
  and the Other, 133–4
  and visibility, 97
  See also queer theory, and identity
IEA Study, 20
ignorance of citizens, 15–6, 17–8
imaginary, curricular, 117
imaginary, global, 117, 120
immigrant experience, 71
"Is Canadian Democracy in Crisis?" (Centre for Research on Information About Canada), 15

Jainism, 29
Japan-Alberta Science/Social Studies Project for Educational Reform (JASPER), 118–22
Johnston, Ingrid, 4
"Judith Templeton," 67, 68, 71–4

Kahne, Joseph, 47–8
Kant, Emmanuel, 129
King, Martin Luther, Jr., 107
Kingwell, Mark, 117
Kymlicka, Will, 121

lawyers, 104–5, 106
Lea, Clarence, 108
learning, 61, 64
Leavis, F. R., 78
Lemme, Ray C., 127–8
Lister, Ruth, 48–9, 52
literature, 4, 76–7, 78, 79
  See also English (language arts)
Little, Edward C., 108
Loutzenheiser, Lisa, 5
Loy, David, 134
lynchings and mutilations, 103, 107, 108, 109, 110

Macintosh, Lori, 5
MacIntyre, Alistair, 64–5, 121
Mahatma Gandhi Foundation, 28–9
Mallo, Greg, 128
"The Management of Grief" (Mukherjee), 4, 67–8
Mangat, Jyoti, 4

Mansbridge, Peter, 16
Marshall, T. H., 33, 34
Massey Lectures, 14
McEwan, Ian, 60
McGill University, Department of Political Science, 21
modernism, 57, 62
Morrison, Toni, 81
Moser, Tilman, 130
Mouffe, Chantal, 1, 52
Mukherjee, Bharati, 4, 67, 80

NAFTA, 25
national identity. *See* identity, national
"National Security Strategy for the United States of America" (NSSUSA), 128
A Nation at Risk, 14
nation concept, 80
New Criticism, 78
Nixon, Jon, 121
Noddings, Nel, 62
normalization of difference, 97
  See also queer theory
Nussbaum, Martha, 55, 59, 60, 64, 118

ontologies, 63
the Other
  protection of, 116
  and queer theory, 97, 98, 99, 100
  and racism, 99, 100
  sacrifice of, 130, 132
  and U.S. policy, 126, 127

Pears, Iain, 58, 59
Phelan, Shane, 100, 101
Pinar, William, 5
political scandals, 16–7
postmodernism, 39
projectivity, 90
public schools
  and curricula of global citizenship, 116, 118
  and good citizenship as a goal, 47–8
  lack of democracy in, 21
  as locus of civic education, 21
  and normalization, 97, 98
  and public policy, 3
  public vs. private spheres of identity, 98–9
  and whiteness (race), 99
public space, 28, 29

queer theory
  criticisms of, 99
  and curricula, 101
  gay and lesbian citizenship, 2, 5
  and identity, 96–7

race, and queer theory, 99–100
racism, 20, 89, 109
  See also lynchings and mutilations
Ragtime (Doctorow), 27
Random House Modern Library, 79
Rape and Faggot (White), 109
Rees, William, 29
Research Unit for Political Economy, 128–9
Richardson, George H., 56–7
Ricoeur, Paul, 55–6, 57, 60, 61
Ryan, Edward, 105

sacrifice of the Other, 130, 132
satyagraha, 29
Sears, Alan, 3, 49
September 11, 2001 attacks (New York), 127
sexual stereotypes, 99–100
Smith, David G., 6, 120
Smits, Hans, 4
social capital, 38
social change, 86, 87–8, 91, 92–3
social cohesion, 20, 36, 38
social life and agency, 87–7
social studies
  aims, 55–6, 62
  curricula, 55, 57
  and disenchantment, 62
  history vs. memory, 58–9
  See also agora
"The Sorrow and the Terror: The Haunting Legacy of the Air India Tragedy," 68
South Africa, and democratic values, 17
Southern Conference for Human Welfare, 109
Southern Regional Council, 109
standardized tests, 49, 62
states rights (U. S.), 107–8, 110
Stein, Janice Gross, 14, 22
stories, 64–5
students
  and agency, 92
  gay and lesbian, 98
  and historical agency, 93
  and multiculturalism, 68–70, 74, 97

Students *(continued)*
  sexual minorities, 97
  views on world citizenship, 118–20
  See also youth
"Student Vote 2004," 16
Sundering of Canada (Bliss), 16

Taylor, Charles, 62, 64
the Teflon self, 64
terrorism, 127
textbooks, 86, 88
Till, Emmett, 109
Toulmin, Stephen, 57
Tupper, Jennifer, 4

UNESCO, civic education policies, 15
United Kingdom, civic education policies, 15
United States
  American biblicism, 125
  foreign policy, 126–8
  history, 88–9
  weapons development, 128–9
  See also Americans; Bush administration (George W.)
Usher, Roland G., 109

values, 31, 32–3, 38
  See also democratic values
Varela, Francesco, 57, 61
voter apathy. *See* alienation of citizens
voting rates, Canada, 18, 19, 25–6
voting rates, United States, 26

Ward, Lester Frank, 108
Weber, Max, 62

Wells, Ida B., 109, 110
Westheimer, Joel, 47–8
What Do Our 17 Year Olds Know? (Ravitch and Finn), 16
Whig narratives, 88–9
Whitaker, Reg, 28
whiteness (race), 4, 5, 74, 99
  See also "Judith Templeton"
White, Stephen, 56, 63
White, Walter, 109
Who Killed Canadian History? (Granatstein), 16
Wilkinson, Lori, 3
wisdom traditions, 29
Woman's International Bar Association, 106
women professionals, 105–6
women, marginalization of, 46–7
Women Lawyers Journal, 106
world citizenship. *See* citizenship, global
world history, cycles of freedom and conquest, 129–9
World System, 129
WTO (World Trade Organization), 25

youth
  and community service, 19, 21
  and consumerism, 29
  and democratic values, 19–20, 25
  diversity of citizen types, 20–1
  political alienation, 18–9, 26
  and racism, 20
  See also students
Youth News Network, 21